THE MONEY ORCHARD©

©2021 by Dennis Zaderaka

Money Making Money
Instead of You Working

THE
MONEY
ORCHARD ©

Money Making Money
Instead of You Working

by

Dennis Zaderaka

Publishing Services provided by Paper Raven Books
Printed in the United States of America
First Printing, 2022

Paperback ISBN= 978-1-7373982-0-2
Hardback ISBN= 978-1-7373982-1-9
Ebook ISBN= 978-1-7373982-2-6

TABLE OF CONTENTS

ACKNOWLEDGMENTS

I want to thank several people for the insights I have gained working as a financial advisor.

Ray Lyne of Lifestyle Giving for the original "Parable of the Apple Tree" when I worked as a volunteer for estate planning and charitable giving seminars in churches. The original parable is in the appendix section of the book.

I want to thank Morgan Gist McDonald at Paper Raven Books for persuading me to write this book and her team for the expert guidance they gave me. With their help, this book is better than I imagined it would be.

I am thankful for the United States of America, where we can build wealth with hard work and our abilities, unlike the countries my grandparents came from.

Most of all, I want to thank all my clients who have allowed me to search for solutions to their unique situations. I am honored that they trusted me to help with their goals and financial life.

HOW TO USE THIS BOOK FOR YOUR INVESTING SUCCESS

If you want to skip ahead and get some ideas immediately, go to Chapter 7 for ways to earn 5% to 10% without a lot of risk.

This book differs from other financial books. It is not explaining facts and details about investments. For detailed investment knowledge, the two primary books you need are on the next page. Almost all other investment books draw from Security Analysis by Benjamin Graham and David Dodd.

I realize most people won't read Graham's 600-page book before they invest. So, I have distilled the information into a practical book anyone can understand and apply. The Money Orchard is a book you can use as a tool to help you invest wisely and successfully.

The way to read this book is to look for clues. Clues to understanding what goes on behind the scenes in financial services and clues you can use to keep your money safe and make it grow. I have tried to keep it simple and practical.

The Money Orchard reveals a different perspective on investing. While most investors and professionals are running in the same direction, The Money Orchard points to a different road you can choose. This book gives a framework to analyze and to question conventional investment "wisdom" that is occasionally wrong. I want this book to give people the idea they can disagree with the investment industry and find a better way.

For example, currently the investment industry builds the entire investment process on a risk profile questionnaire and then prescribes a model portfolio for a fee of 1%. This was a wrap account, but now is called a fee account. The problem: someone's risk profile has nothing to do with what makes a good investment. Even worse, there is no research showing it is possible to measure a person's risk tolerance. The error in the process is they are asking a logical question and applying it to an emotional reaction to future events. It doesn't work.

The goal of The Money Orchard book is to simplify the investment process into steps that anyone can take to reach financial self-reliance, which is often called the American Dream. It can change your life. I wish you incredible financial success.

RESOURCES

The Intelligent Investor, Revised Edition. Copyright © 1973 by Benjamin Graham. New material: Copyright © 2003 by Jason Zweig. HarperBusiness Book (Original 1949.)

Security Analysis by Benjamin Graham and David Dodd. Sixth Edition Copyright © 2009 McGraw-Hill Original 1934.

Winning The Loser's Game Timeless Strategies for Successful Investing, Charles D. Ellis. © 2021

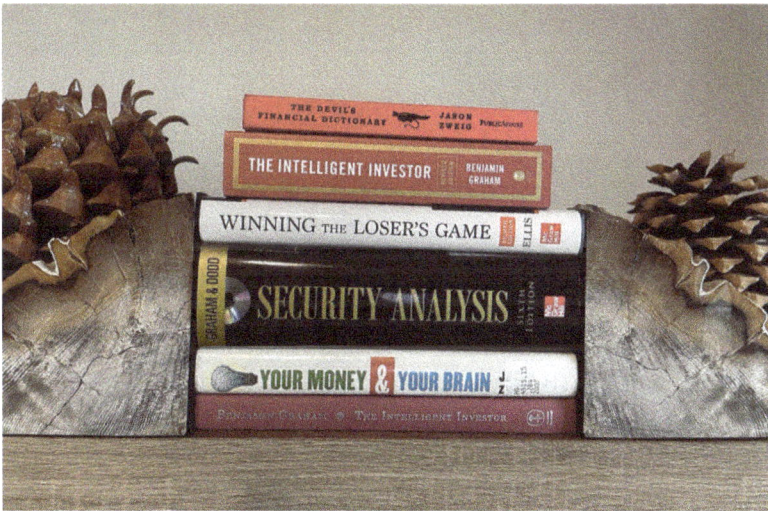

PRAISE FOR THE MONEY ORCHARD

The Money Orchard is a story that will make you think. It is not just a bunch of financial facts. Chapter 7 with 8 ideas to get 5% to 10% is worth the price of this book.

-Tammy Melvold, Bottomline Wealth Management

The Money Orchard is a must-read as it simplifies the world of investing for those just getting started as well as un-complicating investing for those much further along in their quest for investment success. It provides an understanding of investment basics; educates you about investment dangers and highlights the need for a well-grounded investment strategy. The metaphor of an Orchard is brilliant as it simplifies understanding the concepts of savings, investing, and earning income with its down-to-earth comparison to the operation of an orchard. WELL DONE!

-Tom Hansen (Retired Vice Chairman ITW)

The Money Orchard outlines a simple step-by-step approach to successful investing regardless, whether you are a seasoned investor or just starting. It lays out, in clear and concise terms, why "the system" is stacked against everyday people and how to take advantage of reasonable, solid companies rather than using your time and money to enhance Wall Street's bottom line. Over 30 years working with Dennis's guidance and vision has taken me and my husband from inexperienced investors to comfortable retirees, and it can work for you too.

-Margaret Fortuna

Our family is beginning to invest. There are so many choices, it's hard to know which ones are right. The orchard story made the investment world easier for us to understand.

-Nicole and Travis Emerson

HOW I REALLY LEARNED
ABOUT INVESTING

In 1980, I was excited about making money as a rookie stockbroker. My company, Kidder Peabody, one of the oldest firms on Wall Street, took AT&T and railroads public. They sent us to New York for training. I was in the big leagues.

When I came back to Minneapolis, I had a problem. I wanted to use my training to be an advisor and give top-quality guidance to clients. I was trying to sell to people 20 to 40 years older than me. They knew I didn't know anything, and I knew they knew. I had to find customers, so I did everything, including cold calling (I hated cold calling).

After a couple of years, I realized there were two kinds of customers: traders and investors. The short-term traders were young. The investors were older. Traders had very little money. The investors had a lot of money. Each type invested differently. During that time, my understanding of investing changed. People with money weren't trying to make money. They already had money. Their goal was not to lose it and still get a reasonable rate of return.

I decided to specialize in long-term investing for individuals and for 401(k) plans. At one point, my manager told me, "I don't know why you are working so hard on those 401(k) plans. You aren't going to get any. Why do you want all those little accounts?" Within a year, I got my first plan with over 4,000 employees. It was one of the first ones in the US. I also began teaching financial literacy classes as an employee benefit.

The biggest lesson I learned on my journey was that it's okay to challenge conventional thinking and be a pioneer with new ideas. I found two world class investors to learn from.

I found two world class investors to learn from.

At one point, I was lucky enough to learn about John Templeton and his mutual fund. His track record and investment style were impressive and still are. So, I recommended his fund to my clients. Then I learned about another family of funds that followed the same investment philosophy as John Templeton's. They also had a consistent track record of superior performance for decades. My reasons for recommending these mutual funds were what I recommended to my mother and father.

Later, I discovered Warren Buffett, John Templeton and several other managers were students of Benjamin Graham, author of *The Intelligent Investor* (1949) and *Security Analysis* (1934). I became convinced the strategies presented in his book were a superior investment process, which is value investing. Looking at recent history, we see, if investment professionals followed Ben Graham's philosophy of investing, market disasters like 1987, 2000 through 2002, and 2008 probably would not have happened.

The financial service world had (and still has) a very narrow view of investing. Active short-term trading is not really investing, but just moving money around. The odds of long-term success are less than the odds in Las Vegas.

In the early 1980s, there were only about 100 mutual funds compared to over 9,500 now. Most brokers didn't sell mutual funds, but I doubled the amount that our entire office sold the year before. It wasn't very much. I remember the office manager asking me why I was selling all these funds and telling me, "Now you won't be a broker." Another colleague told me, "If you sell funds, you will never see the money again." I was too naïve to understand what they were saying. I was missing an essential piece of the puzzle: active traders produced more commissions. I was blissfully unaware of the two Wall Streets: one for entertainment and the other for serious investing.

In 2021, the tide investors need to swim against is even stronger. The industry has changed a lot. Mutual fund investing has gained in popularity. Active trading has moved to the internet for no visible commission. But investment results have barely changed. Investing is harder and more complex than ever. In fact, I believe the current structure of the industry extracts more value from investors than it adds. There are many investment theories, and not all of them work for long-term success of the individual investor trying to become financially independent.

I offer this book as a tool to help you sift and sort through the ideas in the investment world. It will help you find some gems for your financial success, and you will become less dependent on investment experts. Then you can use banks, insurance, and investment companies to reach your goals, not theirs.

INTRODUCTION

Most of what you hear on TV about investing doesn't work.

Over the course of the 40 years that I have been working with investors, I have discovered that even well-educated people are at the mercy of advertising, marketing, and fancy buzz words. It's financial propaganda. Most people are too busy with their careers and businesses to become an expert in the financial world, which means investors don't have all the facts they need to make good decisions.

Over the years, I developed a metaphor of a money orchard as a tool to translate financial jargon into language anyone can use and understand. It's a story about investments creating your income instead of you working. In short, it's the American Dream. Throughout this book, I will show you how to get income with the same predictability as an apple tree producing apples every year so that you can become financially self-sufficient. It's not complicated because it only requires a slight change in what you already know about investments.

Financial decisions are like getting a puzzle with hundreds of loose pieces; the more money you have, the more complicated the puzzle is. Just like the picture on the box helps put the puzzle together, the money orchard paints a financial picture to help investors see how financial decisions work together.

The Money Orchard

The money orchard shows you how to invest for income.

An orchard of any kind is intentionally growing trees for food production. It is a business. The purpose of every business is to make a profit so it can continue to exist. The reason to grow apple trees is to get apples, not collecting trees. Each task of creating and managing an orchard also applies to investing. In both kinds of orchards (apple or money), it takes knowledge, patience, and time to produce the fruit you want. You would never dig up the trees and move them around.

There are two different economies: the US economy and your economy. And there are two different perspectives in the world of money: yours and the one of the financial service industries. The money orchard shows how you can use the economic system to your benefit and create the American Dream of an abundant income unaffected by bad weather.

The apple tree on the left represents your work, and the apples are your income. A sinkhole signifies debt and taxes. A dark cloud shows there is risk and danger in life. The three kinds of orchard trees symbolize the ways your investments can make money: **protecting** money from losses, **loaning** for interest, and **owning** something that can grow. Each is a metaphor for insurance, banking, and Wall Street. The American Dream is to have investments (or a business) producing the same income as your work.

Dream big dreams.

The purpose of all saving and investment is to create an income. You are not just collecting assets to have a high net worth. This informative guide will help you discover investment strategies very few people know about and help you find money you don't realize you are losing down the sinkhole.

I want to show you a better way to invest by taking everything I've learned over the past four decades and giving you a different perspective from what conventional financial services typically offer. Throughout this book, we'll explore mathematics, academic research, and historical examples as models for better investing.

Part One applies the orchard metaphor to guide you through basic investment principles.

Part Two presents building blocks for creating a successful investment portfolio for growing your money and income.

Part Three provides some practical applications that you can easily understand and follow with confidence. After reading this book, you will have the investment knowledge and tools to gain financial independence, ultimately providing you with a lifetime of safe, predictable income that will allow you to experience as much life as you can dream.

LESSONS FROM THE ORCHARD

Why do you invest? Because you want to:

🍎 Experience a meaningful life.

🍎 Become the person you were created to be.

🍎 Be with the people you want to be with.

🍎 Accomplish all the things you want to do.

🍎 Have peace of mind.

🍎 Make a difference in the world.

🍎 Live a long and healthy life.

🍎 Pass on your values and wealth.

What is the most important idea from this chapter you want to apply to your investments?

_____
_____
_____
_____
_____
_____
_____
_____
_____
_____
_____
_____
_____
_____
_____
_____
_____
_____
_____
_____
_____
_____
_____
_____

PART ONE

PULLING BACK THE FINANCIAL WIZARD'S CURTAIN

Chapter 1

THE LANDSCAPE OF INVESTING

"Only when the tide goes out do you discover who's been swimming naked. When the market goes up and up, everyone looks like an investing genius. It's only when things go sour that you see who has a good long-term strategy."
Warren Buffett

Preparing for Dangers Ahead

Stock Market Crashes

A stock market crash is inevitable. We don't know when it will happen, but we know it will happen. Even though market drops happen regularly, it always seems to be a surprise. From 2000 to 2020, there have been three market declines of 30% to 50%. Just as we recover, another major crisis comes along and there's another crash. Like Charlie Brown, who never figured out that Lucy would pull the football away before he could kick it. Investors never seem to learn how to adjust.

In a market decline, a few investors make a lot of money while most investors lose. During market crashes, people freeze and do nothing or, even worse, panic sell when they should be buying. Investors keep investing the same way and repeat the cycle over and over. The investment world is like stepping into a casino where the deck is stacked against you. Most investors are playing the game without knowing the rules. No one should base their lifestyle and future in this kind of casino. You need to find a better way than riding the stock market roller coaster. The floor traders call it smart money and dumb money. I want you to be smart money.

Inflation

Currently, the debt of the US government is $30 trillion and rising. This is a storm on the horizon that no one seems to see. In the 1980s, we collapsed the Soviet Union by getting them to spend more on their military than their economy could handle. Now we are doing it to ourselves. History is full of examples of out-of-control inflation. The Romans, France, Germany, Argentina, and Zimbabwe are all reminders that uncontrolled government spending ends in disaster. Governmental spending is an enormous problem that leads to higher taxes and inflation. You need to prepare for both.

In money orchard terms, there is a storm on the horizon. The sun doesn't always shine because real life is full of risk. It is too late to build a storm cellar when you see the clouds twisting to form a tornado. You need to protect your assets, your income, and your life. When the sun shines, life goes on smoothly. When the sun doesn't shine, you need a guide that has been on the path before. A guide will point out problems while they are still manageable and will help you navigate difficult events. You can find and fix problems in the book before they become big ones. This is how you can prepare for the inevitable storms.

In early 1922, 160 German marks equaled one US dollar. By November 1923, the currency would depreciate to 4,200,000,000,000 for one US dollar. 4.2 trillion = $1 in 1922 in less than 20 months.

The Financial Service Industry Fails Us

The financial service industry is not in business to educate people about money. Understanding how financial companies work gives you a key to making better investment decisions.

- **Wall Street** is investment banking and corporate finance. The purpose of Wall Street is to raise money for businesses and governments by selling stocks and bonds.
- **Banks** make money by making loans for cars, houses, and businesses and by issuing credit cards. A bank is also a clearinghouse for financial transactions like checking accounts, credit cards, and debit cards. The major business of banks is to make loans.
- **Insurance companies** make money by taking the risks people want to transfer to them, like car accidents, natural disasters, and medical diagnoses. Life is too unpredictable for anyone to accept 100% of potential losses.
- **Financial radio and TV shows** exist to get you to watch advertisements and commercials to sell you products. It's more entertainment than education. Financial media makes more money giving advice than you can make using that advice.
- **Financial planning** may or may not be helpful. I believe in the financial planning process, but sometimes financial planning is a pretense to gather information to sell you more stuff. You need to find an advisor who knows you and helps you in financial decisions in more ways than buying more financial assets. You don't need to be an expert, but you want to know how to work with experts that can work with you.

Only 17 states require high schools to teach at least one class on personal finance. At least 44% of Americans don't have emergency cash to cover a $400 emergency, and 38% of households have significant credit card debt.

While 401(k) plans are an excellent tool for saving, they do not solve all financial issues. Even wealthy people make costly mistakes because their knowledge and experience are limited. In the investment world, much like sports, amateurs will not beat the professionals. Most people do not have time to do all the research necessary to invest successfully. They are too busy with their own careers or business.

Something is wrong with the system when 33% of Americans have no retirement savings. Very few people have enough money to retire and stay retired. The average savings for retirees is a median amount of $152,000. This is almost criminal since there are tangible ways for almost everyone to reach a level of financial security that fits their life. The goal of this book is to peek behind the curtain and reveal the "secrets" of reaching financial self-reliance.

Achieving the American Dream

Almost everyone dreams of earning enough income from a business or investments to achieve financial independence. Money is freedom. Many people don't know how to get there and are intimidated by the process. Most people don't believe they can have investments producing a retirement paycheck instead of their job. Even people with significant assets are afraid they will run out of money. Reasons for uncertainty include limited time, lack of a realistic strategy, false information, conflicting opinions, and lack of a written investment policy and plan. Most people lose money in market declines, and it takes years to recover. Emotions win over facts and logic.

Understandably, people don't totally trust Wall Street. It's risky. There are a lot of financial helpers who extract value from your investments with fees but don't always add value to your investments. Personal finance is like getting the pieces of a puzzle and having no picture to help put the puzzle together. You get bits of information from various financial professionals, accountants, attorneys, financial planners, insurance advisors, employee benefits, mortgage companies, banks, trust companies, investment advisors, books, magazines, and cable TV shows. As a result, your decisions are made in a fragmented manner and don't work together for efficiency.

You want an expanding future to enjoy all the possibilities of life. In the words of financial author Tom Hegna, you need a paycheck and a play check. The paycheck is for surviving, and the play check is for thriving. You need a clear path to financial success. You want control of your own destiny. The tragic result of using the wrong path is you might not retire when you want. Even worse, you might run out of money.

Investing is like being in one of the Chicago commodities pits. When things are going crazy, it sounds like angry bees swarming. The difference between a commodity pit and your investment world is that each pit has only one choice. Many of the choices we face as investors are more complicated and riskier than they need to be. Today, there are at least 9,599 mutual funds, 1,988 ETFs, and 17,079 investment companies. How can you know what's best when the experts themselves disagree? It's a good assumption that not all are good, some are okay, and some are excellent. The experts' advice is on predicting the future that no one can know.

There are hundreds of investment books, dozens of financial shows, endless commercials and countless publications that all claim they have the magic formula to investment riches. How do you know what to choose? How can you be sure you are right? The default choices for most people are (a) choose the biggest firm based on size, (b) go with the biggest brand name, (c) believe the companies that spend the most on advertisements, or (d) do nothing. Another choice is to learn from the most successful investors in history.

The Foundation of Modern Investing: Benjamin Graham

Early in my career, one of my clients loaned me his copy of *The Intelligent Investor* by Benjamin Graham. Legendary financial tycoon Warren Buffett has described it as "the best book about investing ever written" and acclaimed financial journalist Jason Zweig wrote, "Graham was not only one of the best investors who ever lived; he was also the greatest practical investment thinker of all time." In all my years of working in the financial industry, I never learned about this book from any investment service firms. This is an important lesson: financial service companies do not give us all the information we need to make good decisions. I am more than irritated that no investment company or online trading company ever told me about Ben Graham earlier in my investment life.

The best copy of *The Intelligent Investor* is the updated one with commentary by Jason Zweig with a preface and appendix by Warren Buffett. Jason Zweig's commentary on each chapter in The Intelligent Investor covers 70 plus years of investment history after the book was written in 1949. It proves the validity of Benjamin Graham's ideas.

Finding this book helped me understand the financial service industry and how to help my clients invest. It is a foundation for investing, beautifully simple but amazingly comprehensive. *The Money Orchard* applies the principles from Professor Graham's book in ways that you can easily understand and use. My aim is to design and share practical applications based on *The Intelligent Investor* that everyone can use.

The Intelligent Investor Meets The Money Orchard

One test of knowledge is: does it work? Two of Graham's students, John Templeton and Warren Buffett, prove it does. Money magazine named Templeton "arguably the greatest global stock picker of the century." As for Warren Buffett, 60 plus years of incredible investment success using the knowledge gained from Graham confirms his wisdom. Buffett and Templeton applied Graham's theory in real life with outstanding success. There are a few other Graham students who have achieved this kind of consistent success for decades. Not quarters. Not years. Decades. There are a handful of mutual funds with the same investment philosophy and a similar track record over several decades.

Building on the wisdom in *The Intelligent Investor*, this book,

The Money Orchard, goes beyond theory and history and shows practical ways to apply the knowledge that Graham gives us. Graham, the "father of value investing," wrote about investing but not about other important parts of personal finance. *The Money Orchard* applies Graham's investing ideas to the context of your unique financial situation. This will give you a good long-term strategy and proven ways to save and invest based on mathematical principles and historical track records of these three successful investors.

There are no famous day traders who match the wealth and success of Buffett, Templeton, and Graham. Jesse Livermore, a stock trader in the 1920s, was probably the greatest ever. He went from poor to extremely rich and bankrupt at least three times. He ended his life by suicide. If the story of his life doesn't cure you of day trading, nothing will. The main lesson is best described by my commodity trading friend: "The personality that will let you take that amount of risk will keep you doing it until you lose it all."

The orchard metaphor reveals some myths and fallacies of Wall Street and professional money management. For example, Wall Street has a bias towards active trading instead of investing with a long-term view. Why is there a bias towards trading? Let's look behind the Wall Street curtain. The stock market trades at least three billion shares a day, usually more. If the floor specialists make just a penny a share on three billion shares, that makes $30 million a day, $150 million a week, and $600 million a month. In one year, the money generated is over $7.2 billion. Simply processing the electronic flow of pieces of paper called stocks makes a lot of money for Wall Street. Whether the market is up or down, they make money. If the average investor invested according to Graham's principles or followed the example of Warren Buffett, Wall Street would make a lot less money because people would trade less frequently.

The Money Orchard shows that **growing anything takes time and patience**. It is the same for investing, which is hard work and requires dedication. To be a successful investor, you need the four Ts: time, temperament, training, and talent. Buffett and Templeton are perfect examples of people who used the four Ts extremely well. Having humility is also important. As an investor, you need to know you might miss some important information. You need someone who can tell you when you are slightly off track or maybe tell you are wrong. When evaluating investment managers, one question I ask is, "Who tells the boss that he's wrong?" Even Warren Buffett has Charlie Munger, who together have made an incredible team.

How to Use This Book

I want my book to be a catalyst for your ideas. As you read, write down the thoughts that come into your mind. The thoughts you think are more important than the ones I wrote here. It's an investor's "think and do" workbook, like the ones we had in grade school. This orchard story helps you see things differently than the crowd that is usually always wrong. If you are going to succeed, you must do something different from the average investor. Most investors are tossed around the investment seas like a boat without a rudder. Successful investors have knowledge, a policy, and a strategic plan. You will discover the importance in *The Money Orchard*.

Avoid the Bad Ideas

Pension funds and 401(k) plans have a written investment policy as a part of their fiduciary responsibility. It is our firm's belief that individual investors get better results when they have an investment policy. An investment policy is like a fence around your money so you can keep the bad ideas out and find good ideas. Very few investors have a written investment policy.

A company's retirement plan has a written investment policy to guide and restrict the managers to a specific goal to keep the money safe and growing at a realistic rate of return. The same is true for mutual funds. There are two important reasons for having a written investment policy: (1) to avoid disastrous losses and (2) to have a tool for choosing the best investments. You must have a written policy to guide your decisions.

The first step to creating a successful investment strategy is to discover your investment philosophy and what works in the real world instead of theoretical opinions. Based on decades of historical performance, you can find the ones that work best. The history of Wall Street is the history of making enormous amounts of money disappear. An even greater magic trick is getting investors to forget it happened. An investment policy helps you avoid becoming trapped in dead-end investments and find investment success in the real world.

Use your new ideas from this book to write your personal investment policy. It's like writing a business plan, but let's call it **your profit plan**. This will include a To Do list and a Never Do list. It will describe the building blocks and strategies for create your blueprint for financial self-sufficiency. Then you can build your own money orchard portfolio described in the book.

There are many investment styles. You need to know which one or two fit your goals and your investment personality. With your investment policy and plan, you will communicate your wishes with any investment professional. You can hand it to your investment advisor and say, "This is what I want. Please make a proposal on how you would do this." If your advisor gave you this book, you have a good clue you are on the right path.

Having a written investment policy with a clear description of your investment style will help you avoid investment myths and propaganda. Here are a few examples of different investment strategies. Some give more predictable results than others. Your investment policy must fit your investment personality.

Some Investment Philosophies:

- Investor/Speculator
- Long-term/Short-term
- Growth/Value
- Passive/Active
- Top-down/Bottom-up
- Diversified/Non-diversified
- Fundamental Analysis/Technical Analysis
- Market Timing, which is based on predicting the future
- Short-term trading (day trading)
- Option trading
- Hedge funds

Retirement plans and mutual funds have an investment policy.

An advisor who doesn't help you develop a personal investment policy almost borders on malpractice. You wouldn't have confidence in a doctor who didn't take a medical history and do some blood work and other tests. How would the doctor know what to prescribe?

When I work on pension plans or 401(k) plans for companies, they send an RFP (request for proposal) that explains what they want based on their investment policy. If a company retirement plan uses an investment policy, it makes perfect sense for you to use the same process. You deserve an investment policy and strategy that is simple, clear, and realistic.

The Money Orchard gives investors tools and techniques beyond current conventional investment advice. This book helps you believe you can have a self-sustaining income and shows how to build and protect your wealth.

LESSONS FROM THE ORCHARD

Money Orchard Goals:

🍎 You don't want to run out of money.

🍎 You don't want to lose money.

🍎 You want your money to grow.

🍎 You want to increase and protect your income.

🍎 You want to pay fewer taxes.

🍎 You want confidence you are making the right investment decisions.

🍎 You want a future free from financial worry.

What is the most important idea from this chapter you want to apply to your investments?

_____
_____
_____
_____
_____
_____
_____
_____
_____
_____
_____
_____
_____
_____
_____
_____
_____
_____
_____
_____
_____
_____
_____
_____
_____

.

Chapter 2

OVERVIEW OF THE MONEY ORCHARD

"If you don't find a way to make money while you sleep,
you will work until you die."
Warren Buffett

I worked for many years with a client and his wife who were millionaires. The three of us would often talk about all kinds of personal events in their life, such as how their children were doing or their latest vacation. Even though we had good rapport, I noticed the wife would become quiet during the financial discussions and never asked questions or made comments. I knew she was well-educated and intelligent. Since she was an artist, I wondered if using a real-world analogy with visuals would be a better way to communicate about their financial decisions instead of the usual charts and graphs.

During one of our meetings, I drew a picture of an orchard with three trees, the sun, and a dark cloud, and described investment in terms of how an apple orchard works. Her first comment was, "This isn't that hard to understand." Financial projections and accounting spreadsheets communicated nothing to her. It was a foreign language. The orchard metaphor brought her into the conversation about her money and her life. It became a rich discussion of why she was investing instead of a one-sided presentation of technical investment information.

The orchard story helped her see how everything fit together and why. Protecting apples (income) made more sense to her than income planning. Trees representing a portfolio showed the need for diversification, patience, and letting the investments grow. Caring for the orchard and passing it down to their children communicated more than discussing risk management and estate planning. I used the orchard metaphor instead of more technical investment language with other people. Across the board, my clients understood everything better with an orchard picture than conventional investment jargon. When they started using orchard language to talk with me, I realized the power of using the orchard to explain the whole financial planning process.

Traditional financial language describes what something is by using words like bank, insurance, Wall Street, funds, stocks, bonds, and money. Orchard language explains how things work by using words like loaning, protecting, growing, and creating income. Rather than describing investment products, the conversation shifts to what it does and why it is important. Like the picture on the front of a puzzle box, the money orchard gives you a visual picture of your personal finance. It helps you understand the parts and the whole and how all the pieces fit together for your financial success. You will discover unique strategies for building wealth and income that are not typically found in traditional financial planning.

Just as a fruit orchard is the intentional growing of trees for food production, the money orchard story explains intentionally investing to create income. Each of the three trees are symbols of places where you can store money. You can loan your money and earn interest, you can own something that is growing in value, or you can protect your money. The reason you work and invest is to create income.

A well-designed investment portfolio is a proper balance of all three kinds of trees. Each type of tree has a unique and important role in your personal financial situation. The orchard metaphor shows how to design, build, manage, and protect your money. It shows you crucial steps to planting and cultivating this kind of orchard and guides you through some obstacles you will face along the way. If you already have a thriving investment portfolio, the orchard can show how to protect it and continue to grow it. If you are saving and investing, the orchard can help you avoid mistakes and build your investment portfolio more quickly and efficiently.

LESSONS FROM THE ORCHARD

Financial Language	Orchard Language
🍎 Diversify	→ Have different kinds of trees.
🍎 Don't spend principal	→ Don't cut down trees, only eat the apples.
🍎 Avoid debt	→ Your sinkhole is someone else's income tree.
🍎 Be prepared for emergencies	→ The sun doesn't always shine.
🍎 Risk management	→ Build a fence and get crop insurance.
🍎 Manage taxes and reduce fees	→ Look out for worms.
🍎 Cash management and budget	→ Find money you don't know you are losing.
🍎 Investment management	→ Does the business serve people?
🍎 Estate planning	→ Teach your children how to Manage & Protect the orchard while you are alive and after you are gone.
🍎 Financial independence	→ Get income with the same predictability as an apple tree producing apples every year.

What is the most important idea from this chapter you want to apply to your investments?

_____

_____

_____

_____

_____

_____

_____

_____

_____

_____

_____

_____

_____

_____

_____

_____

_____

_____

_____

_____

_____

_____

_____

_____

_____

_____

_____

_____

_____

CHAPTER 3

HOW THE ORCHARD TREES WORK

"Never give up searching for the job that you are passionate about."
Warren Buffett

Two Kinds of Money: Capital and Income

The orchard metaphor shows the difference between the two kinds of money—capital and income—in a way that financial textbooks don't show. Investing is not collecting trees; it's a way to produce income. I think one of the most powerful insights the orchard shows is, there are two kinds of money. One is lifestyle money, which is income. The other is capital, which is owning a business or other financial assets that gives a person their lifestyle money. The orchard metaphor expands investment knowledge by comparing something you already know to something you don't completely understand.

In one financial class I taught, we were discussing capital investment and walking through the importance of living off the dividends and not spending the principal. I wanted to show why spending investments was a bad idea. I asked the class, "If you have an orchard like this, giving you apples for the rest of your life, would you cut down some trees to trade for a car?" My students answered, "No, that would be stupid." I asked them why. They replied, "Because you wouldn't get any more apples." My next comment was, "Don't we do that with our money all the time?" I explained capital produces income. The income can make payments on the car. In the end, you own the car and still have apples for the rest of your life.

The Work Tree

One of my clients was an engineer who owned a business that specialized in cleaning up hazardous waste sites. As we became better acquainted, I learned he had graduated from the Naval Academy and had served in the Navy for 12 years. I asked him why he didn't stay eight more years for the retirement pension. He told me that, in their spare time, the only thing the other officers would talk about was what they were going to do in retirement. He decided that, if retirement was the goal, he was going to do his dream job immediately.

The purpose of money is to live our lives. Sometimes it is important to remind ourselves about this truth. Gaining financial independence serves the purpose of providing you with the freedom to use the talents God gave you. You want to find work that gives you meaning and significance.

Your work tree makes income for your present life and your family. In a perfect world, you have a job that you enjoy by using your unique skills. You earn money when you serve other people with your talent by giving them something they need or want. Essentially, you are exchanging your time, talents, and energy for money. If you want more money, you must provide more service. Your time becomes more valuable by adding knowledge, skills, and experience.

Just like your work needs to serve other people by giving them something they need or want; businesses need to serve people. When you are investing in a business, ask, "Does the business serve people by giving them something they need or want?" If it doesn't, it's not a good business and will eventually die.

The Three Investment Trees

In the money orchard story, we have three kinds of trees: loaning, owning, and protecting. Every investment you can name belongs to one of these three categories. These trees represent an investment portfolio. The orchard is about your future life. Saving money in the orchard is like sending money into the future, because you want to live a good life now and you want a good life in the future.

Protection Tree

You don't want years of hard work to get wiped out by an unseen life event. While life is full of risk, it can be managed or transferred. We pay insurance companies to take some of our risk. We save three to six months of income in a cash reserve for emergencies. Ultimately, we need safety nets for catastrophic losses.

Asset Protection

Later in life, a person will want to pass down their orchard to future generations. Often people think of estate planning as what happens after death. Estate planning is not merely about who inherits the money orchard when you die; it is also about asset protection while you are alive and after you are gone. In a practical way, you are building a fence around the orchard to protect it using trusts. You do this to protect against lawsuits, estate tax, probate, incapacity, medical costs, and divorce. Wills and trusts are just the final step in asset protection.

I was at a farm talking with the owner and his sons about estate planning. He and his two sisters had inherited the farm from their father, and he continued to farm the land just as their father had. One sister kept her portion of the land and made income on the crops. The other sold her portion and now had no income other than Social Security. When he told his son to not sell the land after he died, his son responded, "If it's $15,000 an acre, I'm selling it." The father was visibly irritated. His son just put a dollar value on years of hard work. Worst of all, he had put a dollar amount on his father's way of life and values. The son didn't understand that the land would produce an income for the rest of his life. Later, when we were alone, I asked the owner if he wanted to make sure his grandson could farm the land. His answer was the grandson would love to do that.

Beyond assets, there are orchard values that need to be passed down. Future generations need to be taught how to care for the orchard and respect the hard work it took to plant and cultivate it.

Trusts

John Rockefeller said, "Own nothing and control everything." If you don't own it, you can't lose it. Ownership has limited value. It is the use of the asset that gives it its value. This is what certain types of trusts do. Everything you can do outside a trust you can do in a trust. The trust owns the assets, but you have use of the assets just as you would if there were no trust. If you don't own these assets, no one can sue you to get them.

Insurance

We buy insurance for cars, homes, medical care, and disability. It is not common knowledge that we can insure our income. Life insurance does not replace a person's life, it protects the income for the family if the income earner dies. Annuities are a way to insure a retirement income. Just like farmers buy crop insurance, you can buy crop insurance on your income.

For years, I had a negative opinion about life insurance and annuities. I was a stockbroker. Banks, insurance, and investment firms were separate businesses. They competed for the money, which meant that "the other guys" were the enemy. They couldn't sell the other industries' products like financial services do now. If they got the money, we didn't.

My view of insurance changed when I was 43 and became seriously ill. The doctors couldn't find what was making me sick. I was weak and extremely fatigued. Even a second opinion from the Mayo Clinic could not determine what was wrong. I now joke that I was so sick I was afraid I wasn't going to die.

I worried about my family. I had a wife and two young daughters, ages two and nine. I remember thinking, "If this is the end of the trail for me, it's okay. I've had a great life, but I don't want to leave them." I worried about how they would survive financially. I remember waking up at night in a panic. I asked my wife if the disability and life insurance policies were paid. This went on for several weeks. Finally, I felt comfortable in knowing that, if I was dead are, they would be in good shape financially. At that point, I relaxed and could concentrate on getting better. That is when I realized that while I bought life insurance for them, I also bought it for myself. I had crop insurance on my income. If I died, my family would have money to live. I would leave them a money orchard.

Loan Tree

There are a variety of ways to loan money. A CD or money market account is loaning your money to a bank. A bond is a loan to an organization, like US treasury bonds, municipal bonds, corporate bonds, or a bond mutual fund. Your savings or checking account is a loan to the bank. When you invest in annuities or certain kinds of life insurance, you are loaning your money to an insurance company. Banks and insurance companies are professional managers of their investment portfolios, so it is another way to get professional money management.

You need to understand how banks work so you can see that their goals and your goals are not the same. You want to avoid paying interest. They want you to pay interest. Banks make money by making loans to businesses and consumers. The bank is not there to help you make money. They make money by earning interest from the loans you take out so you can buy a car, purchase a home, get an education, or finance a business. (These are wise uses of debt; we'll discuss unwise uses of debt later in the chapter.)

Once, I worked at a bank creating retirement plans for the business customers. Sometimes people would complain when the bankers wouldn't approve their loan request. What I learned from sitting in on the loan committee was they were getting free business consulting. There was something the bankers did not like in the business plan. I would explain to the business owner that they were getting free advice that they could use to improve their business. If the bankers see something negative, you want to know what the bank doesn't like. That way, you can avoid the problem the bank sees. If you talk to them and make some changes, they might be more comfortable making the loan and your business could avoid a big mistake.

A bank does not want to make a bad loan; they don't want your house or your car. The president of the bank where I worked, who was also my friend, once told me the story about the only repossession he had ever had to make. A few days before Christmas, a business owner came to the bank and handed over the keys to his home; an employee had embezzled money from the business. As the president and officer of the bank, he was forced to take their house because it was pledged as collateral for the loans. He also knew the family had a son who was dying from cancer. He told me that, when he went home, he spent the night crying. He said, "I decided I never wanted to experience that again. If I have a doubt that someone can pay the loan, I won't approve it."

Own Tree

The own tree is the most exciting to talk about and use, but it is also the most dangerous. We can own a part of a good business by buying stocks from businesses all over the world. We can share in the growth and the income that business produces. Investors can buy one company or buy a managed portfolio like a mutual fund that owns many businesses. The diversification this provides can lower the risk of owning just one company. The beautiful thing about owning a share of a good business is that someone with $100 gets the same return as someone with $10,000,000.

There are lots of things to own. Each one requires some knowledge and skill. You can make money by owning businesses, real estate, land, apartments, office buildings, and farms. Gold, silver, other precious metals, minerals, and commodities are another way to own something of value. Art or rare coins are also assets you can own. What is common to all of them is you must know what you are doing if you don't want to lose.

Investment banking, commonly known as Wall Street, is how we can own a piece of the world's most successful businesses. We can grow our money this way. I believe the words "investing in the stock market" are the wrong way to describe investing. The stock market refers to indexes like the S&P, Dow Jones, and NASDAQ. Indexes are a measurement tool for the US economy. It makes little sense to invest in a measurement tool. Investing in a part of a good business, does. When the stock market index is going down, good businesses can continue to grow and pay dividends.

The S&P 500 index measures the economy represented by 500 stocks. The sales pitch is that 85% of managers don't beat the market, so you should buy the index fund. Instead, we should ask, "who are the 15% who do beat the market?" Buying all 500 stocks of the index seems counterproductive. The best-performing 250 stocks get offset by the worst-performing 250 stocks.

A practical application for investing is to ask these questions:

- Is this a good business?
- Does it serve people by giving them what they need or want?
- Does it solve a problem?
- Does it have good management?

If the answers to these questions are yes, then it is probably a good business and worth the risk of investing. Your goal is to create an income-producing portfolio using all three trees.

Dangers and the Sinkhole

There are dangers that threaten your orchard. You need to watch out for obstacles and dangers to financial success because life is full of risk. One of the greatest dangers is the sinkhole, which is more like a black hole for money. The sinkhole represents debt. Just like compounding interest makes money grow, debt compounds into more debt. It is important to protect the trees from an ever-expanding sinkhole. The sinkhole is a debt from credit cards, car loans, student loans, and any kind of debt on which you pay interest. You should always remember that **your sinkhole is someone else's loan tree**. This is the reason you get credit card applications almost every week. Your debt is someone else's income.

There are foolish uses of debt and wise uses of debt. A home mortgage is a wise use and is one major exception to Warren Buffett's debt-averse nature. He has said that homeownership makes sense for people who plan to stay in one place and that the **30-year mortgage is an excellent financial tool**, especially because if rates go down, you can always get another loan. He said, "It's a one-way renegotiation. It is an incredibly attractive instrument for the homeowner."

Another danger is stress. Stress is a normal part of life, and some kinds of stress, like exercise, are good. Other stresses, like illness, lack of sleep, difficult working environment, and chronic relationship problems, are bad for our health. Financial stress is a stress that can be reduced and sometimes avoided. The orchard image helps you see the big picture and find ways to reduce possible dangers.

Let's apply this to investing. The economy and the stock market ebb and flow. When the economy is down, most people sell at the bottom. Everyone knows you buy low and sell high. Why do most people do the opposite? It is because of stress and fear.

Investors know they should use market declines as a buying opportunity. But the pain is so great they cannot take it any longer. They just want to get rid of the pain, so they sell. Logically, it is the wrong thing to do. This is financial suicide. But the stress adds so much pressure, it is almost impossible to not give up.

LESSONS FROM THE ORCHARD

The money orchard adds unique contributions to the conversation about personal finance. The orchard story:

- Helps you find money you don't know you are losing so you can invest.

- Shows the mistake of cutting down a tree (spending capital) and losing apples (income) forever.

- Connects your sinkhole (debt) to the loan tree (someone else's income tree), which shows both are compounding interest but in different directions.

- Shows your sinkhole could become an orchard.

- Changes the investment goal from investing in the stock market to buying a good business.

- Highlights the right question for finding a good business: does the business serve people by giving them something they need or want?

- Shows that people and businesses make money by serving people. Money is a byproduct of service.

- Shows how capitalism is not evil; it's money-making money by giving people what they need and want.

🍎 Teaches there are two kinds of money: capital and income.

🍎 Provides some unique ways to reposition assets for safety, growth, and income.

🍎 Emphasizes the importance of protecting the orchard and the apples.

🍎 Teaches that personal finance and corporate finance have different goals that rarely match.

🍎 Reframes investment goals from accumulating assets to creating income.

What is the most important idea from this chapter you want to apply to your investments?

_____
_____
_____
_____
_____
_____
_____
_____
_____
_____
_____
_____
_____
_____
_____
_____
_____
_____
_____
_____
_____
_____
_____
_____
_____

CHAPTER 4

THE THREE ESSENTIAL
BUILDING BLOCKS

"Investors should be skeptical of history-based models. Constructed by a nerdy-sounding priesthood using esoteric terms such as beta, gamma, sigma, and the like, these models tend to look impressive. Too often, though, investors forget to examine the assumptions behind the models. Beware of geeks bearing formulas."
Warren Buffett

Why do so few people achieve financial independence? I spend a lot of time thinking about the answers to this question. If I and other financial advisors can prove mathematically that doing certain things will help people be financially successful and replace their work income with investment income, then what prevents more people from reaching financial freedom?

I teach various financial classes offered by employers as an employee benefit. For one company, I taught pre-retirement classes twice a year for seven years. This experience of meeting thousands of people from many companies and all levels of education and income has given me a valuable perspective on what works and what does not.

For quite some time, I was stuck using the language of the traditional financial service world. I spoke in financial jargon. It is a language that most people don't fully understand. They understand the words but not the full meaning. It's like taking people to a foreign country and expecting them to understand what everyone is saying. Investing needs to be explained in ways that help investors confidently choose what's best for them.

Three Crucial Steps

There are three steps to having a money orchard where your money creates your income. First, you need to WANT an orchard. Second, you need to BELIEVE you can have an orchard. Third, you need to KNOW HOW to design, build, manage, and monitor your orchard.

Financial service companies talk about just one of these areas: how to do it. They design and sell financial products in a transactional relationship, either a fee-based transaction or commission-based transaction. This is true for car loans, home loans, individual stocks or bonds, mutual funds (which include closed-end funds, open-end funds, index funds, and ETFs), life insurance, car and home insurance, managed money funds, wills and trust documents, CDs, checking accounts, and trust companies. These decisions are fragmented and disconnected from other transactions. In short, everything ends up being reduced to buying a product.

The first financial classes I taught focused on different investment choices. I spent most of the class time showing how to invest. Teaching knowledge about investing is just "information transfer" but is not practical or always useful. Most people don't believe they can achieve this life-changing goal of financial freedom. Then one class showed me I was missing the most important piece. People can want an orchard that gives them an income while they sleep. They can learn how to invest. I learned I need to help them believe they can do it.

This happened when I was teaching a financial class for a US Army Reserve unit. It is important for soldiers to be financially stable. If a soldier gets into financial difficulty, he or she might lose security clearance and be discharged. During the class, the questions the soldiers asked revealed they wanted a money orchard and understood there are ways to get a money orchard. However, their questions were not about how to do it. What I realized from the questions and comments was they did not believe they could do it. No matter how I answered the questions, I could not get them to picture themselves living in the future with a money orchard that could produce the income they needed to live.

This is when I realized I had discovered the biggest obstacle to financial self-reliance. That barrier is believing you can have a money orchard. In my 40 years working as a financial advisor, I have seen people who were making a million dollars a year with little savings and few investments. I have also seen people who made $50,000 a year create a million-dollar orchard for themselves.

I learned the people who wanted to build wealth wanted it intensely. They believed they could achieve it. They worked to learn how to do it. Success requires that we put all three pieces together of wanting, believing, and knowing how.

Wanting an orchard is the easiest part. The hardest part is believing you can have it. Showing people how and what kind of orchard to build is the easiest part. Showing how is where the financial industry starts and stops. If people don't believe they can build an orchard, they won't do the things necessary to make it happen.

Wanting

Many wealthy people started out life in the middle class or even in poverty. What is the "secret" that helped them achieve financial wealth when most others didn't? One was deciding they wanted financial success. They worked hard and sacrificed. It didn't happen by accident. They earned it.

The important first step in creating your orchard is to decide you want it with an intense desire. It must move from wishing to wanting and then setting goals with an intense desire to do what is necessary to reach your goals. We are discussing money, but the purpose of money is creating your life.

Believing

One of many obstacles to financial independence is advertising that tells you what you should want. Their goal is to get your dollars out of your pocket into theirs. They create dissatisfaction in your life and claim their product will make you happy. Most consumer purchases are impulse decisions. Marketing people know this fact and use it against you. Instead, you can use the powerful psychology behind advertising to your advantage. Think of it as financial judo. TV commercials influence your behavior. Write a commercial to sell yourself the future life you want.

When you are in bed trying to go to sleep, think about this question. If I have all the money I need to live, how will I spend my life? Just like the commercial shows how happy you are when you have their product, imagine how happy you are when you see your dreams becoming real.

Dream a little. Imagine your life free from financial worry. See the difference you will make in the lives of people you love. Imagine how you will grow into the person you want to be, experiencing all the things you want out of life. Visualizing your future in this way is like playing a movie in your mind. If you give your brain the assignment to seek this kind of life, it will find a way to reach it. The book The New Psycho-Cybernetics is a great resource that explains how your brain works to reach the goals you assign it. [1]

Gain Confidence

Believing is the hardest of the three steps. You want to create an orchard that gives you the income for this kind of life, but it's hard to believe that it's possible. Consider this question: if other people can do it, why can't you?

---

1 Maxwell Maltz, M.D., *The New Psycho-Cybernetics* (Prentice Hall Press, Paramus, NJ, 2002), edited and updated by Dan S. Kennedy.

One reason is you don't know how to do it or have never seen it done. I think the biggest obstacle many people face is a lack of confidence that they can do it. You need confidence that what you are doing will succeed. You need to find people around you who will support your belief that you will reach your goals. Other people's negative opinions are the most destructive cancer that prevents people from creating a money orchard. They don't believe they can do it, and they don't want you to do it either. Most people will always find a reason something cannot or will not happen. I am suggesting your thoughts should be: "Thank you for showing me what won't work. Now I am going to find how to make it work." History is full of examples of people who defied what everyone "knew" was reality. People once believed the Earth was flat and the center of the solar system. They believed no one could run a mile in under four minutes until Roger Bannister did. Conventional wisdom is often wrong.

I can show you mathematically that getting to a million dollars is possible. I can show you other people have done it. I can give examples of ordinary people who have done it. I can give you small steps you need to take to succeed. I can even help you design a blueprint that fits you. What I don't know how to do is block all the negative voices telling you cannot do it. Negative emotions are mental prisons. We all have them. We tell ourselves that it can't be done, that it's impossible, that it's too good to be true. Maybe other people can do it, but not me. I want to help you break through this mental barrier.

My mother's parents came from England and Ireland. They were agricultural laborers for centuries. My mother was born in the

US, but she still carried the mental image of being part of the British lower class. I remember her telling me when I was a small boy, "We can't have that because we are poor people." I remember thinking, "Let's quit being poor people." Fortunately, I was smart enough to not say it out loud.

Visualize Reaching Your Goal

If other people can succeed financially, why do you think you can't? It is easy for people to want financial independence. It is relatively easy to build a plan that people can follow with confidence based on mathematical principles and facts, not guesswork. I have found my actual job is helping people believe they can have financial independence and support them on their journey. Of course, you need an intelligent strategy and good investments, but believing and sticking to the strategy is the hard part.

So how do you create the belief that you can have an orchard? Understanding how the mind works is the first key step. When I was a stockbroker on Wall Street, one of the new guys had been an Olympic ski coach. He asked me what I did to succeed. I told him about the book Psycho-Cybernetics by Maxwell Maltz and how I was using those concepts about the mind being a goal-seeking mechanism or a problem-solving system. If you give it a task or a problem to solve, it subconsciously works on the problem. It's like an automatic success mechanism.

One technique in this process is visualization. We imagine ourselves as if we were already successful in reaching our goal. This former ski coach told me he used this principle with his skiers all the time. Since they couldn't use the course the day before the race because the practice would wreck the course, he had them walk down the side of the course, imagining what they would do at each stage. He also added another dimension, telling the skiers to imagine how they were feeling at each turn on the course.

You become what you think about. Your mind finds a way to make your thoughts become a reality. This works both with positive and negative thoughts. In short, your thoughts expand your life or restrict it. I know this sounds like pop psychology, but I've seen it work for myself and other people. I am asking you to have an open mind and consider it as a possibility.

Besides visualization, there is another key to cultivating the groundwork for belief in your own success: you need people who inspire you. All professional sports teams have a manager and coaches. It is interesting that the best athletes in the world still need a coach, a trainer, or a manager. At a professional level, all the players have natural talent and remarkable skills. The difference between winning and losing is an intense belief in their minds that they will win. You are more likely to succeed if you have a few friends with similar goals and people in your life who believe in you.

Knowing How

There are many books with detailed explanations about how to invest. Parts Two and Three of this book will have suggestions as well. There are some basic guidelines to follow. They are simple but not simplistic.

A few years ago, one of my friends and I were teaching an investment class at a company. We explained the four rules of investing. When we were back at the office, he pulled out a guitar and sang it to the tune of "Blue Suede Shoes."

The four rules of investing:

1. Don't lose money.
2. Make money grow.
3. Eliminate taxes.
4. Hire a pro.

Rule #1: Manage risk and don't lose money. We discussed earlier how dangers and risk are a part of life that can damage or destroy anyone's orchard. In real life, everyone makes mistakes and poor decisions. Life in your money orchard will be the same. Once you've reached your retirement income goals, there is no reason to keep putting your money at risk. If you make more money, it probably will not change your life. If you lose money, it will change your life forever. When you lose money, it could have been compounding for years.

Success in any business or activity is a series of good decisions and adjusting mistakes. Sometimes you will make mistakes, but the idea is to keep them small and learn from them. Be kind to yourself. Judge your success by progress, not perfection. Perfection is an impossible goal. It's like chasing the horizon; you will never catch it. It only causes frustration, even when you are achieving outstanding success. Many small decisions slowly will get you to your goal. Remember the story of the tortoise and the hare: steady plodding is kind of boring, but it will get you where you want to be.

Rule #2: Make money grow. You need proven investment strategies. Using mathematical calculations and compounding interest to chart the right path forward, you can succeed. Follow a proven path. Study and do what the most successful investors have done.

Rule #3: Minimize taxes. Taxes are a big drain on your income and the growth of your money. There are legal ways to avoid or reduce taxes so your orchard can grow faster.

Rule #4: Hire a pro to guide you. In sports, even the highest performing athletes hire a trainer. In a later chapter, I will talk about ways we often fool ourselves. An expert guide can help you see what is real and what is not. Everyone has blind spots. We all need someone who can help us see things from another perspective, much like seeking a second opinion when making an important medical decision.

With investing, I like the word "guide" because I do not think people need a financial coach or manager. When you are looking for a financial advisor, you want a guide who has traveled the path successfully. Together, you will create a plan that you can understand and follow confidently. Your guide should help you stay on a path to financial freedom, regardless of outside events. The job of the professional is to bolster your confidence that you are on the right path and to warn you when you deviate from the path you planned charted at the beginning.

LESSONS FROM THE ORCHARD

🍎 Want a money orchard and temporarily delay other things you want.

🍎 Create the belief that you can achieve financial success.

🍎 Learn how to invest and follow the four rules.

*What is the most important idea from this chapter you want to apply
to your investments?*

_____

_____

_____

_____

_____

_____

_____

_____

_____

_____

_____

_____

_____

_____

_____

_____

_____

_____

_____

_____

_____

_____

PART TWO

Building an Investment Portfolio

CHAPTER 5

THE SEEDS FOR INVESTING

"Don't save what is left after spending;
instead spend what is left after saving."
Warren Buffett

The best strategy for saving I ever came across was from an average middle-class couple. They decided how much income they wanted for retirement income and then calculated what they needed to save every month to achieve their goal. Whatever was left, they spent on their lifestyle. They avoided credit cards and paying unnecessary interest. By investing for 35 years, they reached their desired income at age 65. They prepared for their future life first, then used what was left to live in the present. This seems to me to be a brilliant strategy.

Traditional financial planning calls this budgeting, cash management, or pay yourself first. I prefer to call it a spending plan. Budgeting seems negative and living a life of restriction. A spending plan gives the feeling of having a choice and control over my life. Keeping track of where you spend money lets you know if you are making progress or falling into the sinkhole.

One way of keeping track of your expenses is to use one credit card or debit card to pay for everything. That way, you get a summary of your expenses at the end of every month. Another way that I restrict my spending is to pay with cash; it's easier to save when I can physically see my money disappearing.

It is important to know what your expenses are and to have an inventory of what your financial assets are. When my father-in-law died, we found a stash of net worth statements that he made every December for almost 50 years. He kept track of where he was financially to check if his money was growing. With a high school education, he had enough financial sophistication to plant and cultivate his own money orchard.

John Templeton, founder of the Templeton Foundation, was a brilliant investor. If there was an investment hall of fame, he might be number one. He grew up during the Great Depression. After college, he started investing. He and his wife decided to live on one salary and use the rest to invest. He once said, "There were better stock analysts than me, but the difference was I had some money to invest in my ideas; they didn't have money to invest in their ideas." The result of choosing to save instead of buying everything he wanted was that he later had money to get all the things he wanted.

Saving Is the First Step to Investing

Saving money is difficult. One fact we can't escape is that people who don't save work for people who save. Without savings, there will never be an orchard. You prepare the soil with an investment policy and start the apple trees with savings. Very few people have excess money left over. What we earn with our work seems to evaporate with normal living. Between rent or mortgage, utilities, taxes, fees, interest payments, medical bills, children, and recreation, the biggest problem to solve is finding the money to save.

One important starting point of investing is saving a little money consistently. It is better to save $50 a month instead of an overly ambitious goal like $500, which sets you up for failure. We live in a consumer-driven economy. There is a powerful bias to encourage spending. About two-thirds of the US economy is consumer spending. If everyone saved as much as they should and avoided credit card debt, our economy would collapse because spending would be reduced. Your retirement funds would be bigger. When you buy something at a store, they ask if you would like to open a store credit card and get 10% off everything you buy. Why? Because they know they will sell you more stuff. Consumers buy 30% more with a credit card than with cash. It might be more profitable to skip the 10% discount.

From my experience as a financial planner for 40 plus years, I believe budgets don't work for most people, and I think I know why. Budgets give a logical plan for the way you ought to spend, but people spend money on what they want. Wants win over ought almost every time. 90% of consumer purchases are impulse spending. This is a hard battle to fight, as every mother who has stood in the grocery checkout line with small children looking at the candy rack knows.

The Money Orchard

Everyone Has the Same Struggle

Saving is a struggle for everyone, regardless of income. Making more money is not the solution. One of my clients made a million dollars a year as a manufacturer's rep. He had very little in savings and credit card interest of $50,000 a year. Other than a small retirement account of $100,000, a big house, and luxury cars in the driveway, he had little to show for his hard work. There are many examples of people who have earned or inherited sizeable sums of wealth and then lost it because of uncontrolled spending. They did not learn how to say no. Instead, they spend like they will always make the same income forever.

In contrast, another client, who was a truck driver who never made an annual income over $25,000 had $500,000 in his investment account created by wise investments. He started by investing $10,000 in one convertible bond of a small growing company that converted to a rapidly growing stock. When I met him, his orchard was earning more than his work income. Forty years later, his investment portfolio is worth a few million dollars.

As a general pattern, I notice people start thinking about retirement seriously around the age of 45. That was true for me, too. When I was around that age, I thought about how much money I had made since I was 25. My next thought was, "Where is it?" I got a clue when I moved. I was selling, giving away, or throwing away lots of things that I'd bought over the years. I remember thinking I wished I had the money instead of all this junk. Then, looking ahead, I realized I didn't want to say the same thing in another 20 years.

During your lifetime, millions of dollars will flow through your checkbook. From age 25 to age 65, here are some examples if you earn:

$25,000 for 40 years is ➜ $1,000,000

$50,000 for 40 years is ➜ $2,000,000

$100,000 for 40 years is ➜ $4,000,000

Your goal is to move some of your money from your present lifestyle into your future lifestyle. You want to live well now, but you also want to live well in the future. Saving is for future spending. Let's assume you want an orchard so that at age 65 you can retire with $1,000,000. It will give you an income of at least $50,000 a year. That, plus Social Security, provides a good retirement for most people.

There are several ways your money orchard is losing apples and maybe even trees. Since the losses are often small or slow, they may not seem significant and are easy to miss. One of the biggest mistakes people make is thinking a little bit of money is just a little bit of money. A penny on the ground is just a penny. Imagine if you were to put the stopper in your bathtub, turn on the water at a drop per minute, and go away for several days. You would come home to an overflowing bathtub. Paying attention to small amounts of money can add up to at least one tree in your orchard.

How to Stop Money Drains

I am not comfortable telling you how to live your life and how to spend your money. How you spend your life and money is your choice. There are financial radio and TV shows that recommend what I would consider a severely restrictive life. I don't like this approach. I don't want to eat beans and rice, never go out to eat, and make coffee at home to economize. I don't think you need to, either.

Our family went to Disney World when my daughters were 6 and 12 years old. If we never made that trip, our children would not have been harmed. Still, it was a family experience that money can't measure. That is the reason I work and want a money orchard. I want to have an income so I can choose the lifestyle I want. I want an income so I can experience an expanding life, not a shrinking life. I don't want to be limited because I ran out of money.

Few of us have all the money we need for everything we want. We must make choices. If I have $10 and there are four things I want, I have to say no to three things. We decide what is most important. We all spend money on things that are important to us, and these things often cannot be justified by logic or math, as much as we might try.

Let's make a slight shift in the way we think about money. We only have so much time and a certain amount of energy. We exchange some of our time and energy for money. My dad would always talk about how much time he had to work to buy something. Sometimes I think this way when I buy something. Let's use getting a cup of coffee at Starbucks as an example. If a person makes $15 an hour, it takes 30 minutes of work to pay for it because they are paying with after-tax dollars.

At least one-third of their earnings go to state, Federal, Social Security, and Medicare taxes first. One technique for saving money is to ask yourself: how much of my life am I willing to spend to get this? Sometimes the answer will be, I don't want this that badly when you see it from this perspective.

What I am suggesting is you make the goal of creating investments just as important as other choices. The suggestions below are a few ideas of how to find money to save. You will have your own ideas.

The Money Vampires

Let's talk about money vampires. The first and biggest drain on your money is taxes. The more you make, the bigger percentage they take, assuming your income is at least $50,000 a year. You are in the lowest bracket. It increases as you earn more money.

Federal tax	12%–37%
Social Security	6.2%
Medicare	1.45%
State average	5%
Minimum Total	**24.65%**

In the lowest possible tax bracket with an income of $50,000, 24.65% or **$12,325 of your income is lost**. That's almost a quarter of your income. This leaves you with $37,675 for your living expenses. In addition, you also must pay sales taxes, property taxes, gasoline taxes, cell phone taxes, and in some places, city income taxes and even a tax on savings and investments. The tax drag depends on the state you live in. The amount of the money you lose to taxes can be 50%. No wonder it is hard for most people to get ahead financially.

Think about how much money that would be if you could invest it. The long-term price of taxes is the amount it could grow into. I believe a good financial advisor can make more money for you managing your taxes than they can by investing. Of course, you want both. We will explain later the use of Roth IRAs and deductible retirement accounts to limit taxes.

In retirement, you only need to replace your income with $37,675 on a tax-free basis to live, which is an equivalent to $50,000 taxable income. Why replace a taxable $50,000 so you can continue to pay taxes to net $37,675? One goal in retirement is to have mostly tax-free income.

Managing Taxes to Create Tremendous Wealth

It is possible for people to avoid paying some taxes. This would give you thousands of dollars in the future. Remember, if you don't pay the tax, you continue to make money using tax money. The idea is to avoid taxes legally, not evade. Evading sends you to jail.

Lost Opportunity Cost: A Practical Application

During my first year as a stockbroker, I came into the office early to read some research in the company's library. I saw a closed-end mutual fund that was a venture capital firm selling at a discount for $8. (A closed-end fund sells on the stock exchanges and can sell at a discount or a premium.) I knew this was a great investment. It owned several startup companies, one of the computer companies was worth more than $17. It was like buying one and getting the rest for free. I invested in that fund. Then, every time I bought something, I thought about how it wasn't just the $100 I was spending; it was the $100 could buy that stock and what it could grow into. I started thinking about the cost of anything I bought in terms of the money my money could make.

If you have an investment that could grow by at least 20%, the cost of spending $100 today in three-years is $200, in six years $400, and in eight years $800. The ultimate price is $800 and all the income that $800 will produce. The question you should ask yourself is, "Which do I want more?" Sometimes the investment opportunity wins. Sometimes the thing you want to buy wins. Both are okay. The money orchard is a tool to evaluate your decisions. It helps you to consider whether you want the money to work in your orchard.

Make Savings Automatic

In much the same way that companies set up automatic deduction from your checking account to make sure they get paid every month, you can use this same strategy to your advantage as another financial judo move. Set up an auto draft payment into your investment account. That way, you can make sure you are building your money orchard. It doesn't have to be a lot of money. Start small, even if it is only $25 a month. Another automatic saving choice is using the payroll deduction into the 401(k) at work. Hopefully, you have a Roth 401(k) option. Even if you invest just $6,000 a year into a Roth, in 30 years, you will be close to having a good orchard.

There are plenty of ways to save incrementally with small changes in your lifestyle. Americans love to eat out. It is entertainment and nourishment. When I was in graduate school, I remember calculating how much I spent at restaurants. When I came up with over $500 a month, I was shocked. I was only going out two times a week, plus a few lunches. It is hard to go to any restaurant without spending at least $40 or $50 once you include drinks, appetizers, and desserts. These small decisions add up to a bigger bill quickly. Not that you must stop eating out. One small step might be to eat out one time less per week. That decision alone could easily add up to $100 or $200 a month. Younger people can start saving small amounts, even $10 a month. Just like in weightlifting, you don't start lifting 200 pounds the first day of your training. You start with a lighter weight and gradually add more as you get stronger.

Another strategy is to go on a spending fast. I tried this by having a contest with myself to see how little money I could live on for one month. One way I did it was to only eat food we made at home. The result was that we ate healthier and better-quality meals. You could also only pay with cash for a month. It's much harder to spend when you hand over your money and watch the amount in your wallet dwindle to nothing.

At the end of one of my financial literacy classes, a student told me about her experience with saving. She started saving $25 a month and buying a few shares of a few companies she liked. As she received raises, she kept her standard of living the same so she could invest more. Today, she's worth several million dollars and no longer needs to keep her standard of living low. Once you see some success, it will motivate you to continue saving and to increase the amount you are investing.

Major Money Drains

The first ideas in this chapter are about how to save inch by inch. Now I want to discuss making progress mile by mile.

Homeownership

One of the biggest financial decisions is homeownership. For many people, this is the largest financial transaction in their lives and involves hundreds of thousands of dollars. When you consider the cost of commissions, moving expenses, and fees, you could easily spend $40,000 to $50,000. Selling a $300,000 house with 5% commission and buying another house extracts $15,000 on both properties, not including other fees and expenses. Every move you make costs about half an orchard over 30 years. Usually, you don't notice the drain of money because the house appreciates in value.

I remember the first house my wife and I bought. The agent was a friend of mine and did an excellent job of advising us. He told us that there were more costs to owning a home than the price of the house and property taxes. The rule of thumb he used for the additional costs of homeownership was about half the cost of the house (furniture, drapes, rugs, landscaping, and more). The other thing he suggested was to buy the smallest house in a good neighborhood, since it would sell easily if we moved.

Property Taxes

I lived in Illinois for 34 years. One motivation to move to Arizona was to reduce my property taxes, which in Illinois was $14,000 a year for a three-bedroom house. I sat down and added up all my property taxes for 34 years. They totaled $286,000, which is an average of $8,429 a year. If I invested $8,429 each year at 6%, I would now have $878,000. Now I live in Arizona where $14,000 a year almost pays the mortgage and tax on the same size home. You will pay property taxes somewhere, but you can choose where you live and find lower tax rates.

Mortgages

One of the most common banking mistakes people make is opting into a 15-year mortgage instead of a 30-year mortgage. As you pay down a 30-year mortgage, you are paying the loan off over the years with discounted dollars because of inflation. Banks know this, so they created variable rate loans and 15-year loans. That way, they get their money back more quickly and reduce their interest rate risk. When interest rates are low (like they are now), you want to lock in the low rate for as many years as possible.

Another mistake people make is paying their mortgage with extra payments. They have the goal of a paid-off house. A better goal is to **be able** to pay off the house but invest the extra payment in quality income or growth investments. A great idea is to put it into a Roth IRA that grows in tax free and comes out tax free.

What if you found money you didn't know you were losing?

Your money to works inefficiently because of taxes, fees, and inflation. By concentrating on the efficiency of your money, you can increase your wealth without using aggressive investments. Paying attention to little bits of money can add up to hundreds of thousands of dollars. A good CPA or financial advisor usually can find at least $5,000 of waste in most people's spending.

Let's imagine you are 35 years old, and you or your spouse will retire in 30 years. With the help of a financial advisor, you discover that you're wasting $5,000 a year. If you invested the $5,000 each year at a 5% yield in a tax-free account, at the end of 30 years you would have an additional $332,000. That's another orchard tree. Your income from that tree is $16,600 at 5% per year. This is a shift in thinking from the present cost to the amount of future income you are losing.

Let's think about how you can find money you don't know you are losing. In the class I taught for the Army Reserve unit, one soldier told me they saved every paycheck from their reserve duty and invested it for retirement. Another one told me about their hobby of photography, which they used to make a little extra income so they could invest.

Most people think, 'It's only a dollar.' When you go to a restaurant or stop at a gas station and add a soft drink or coffee, you don't even give it a second thought. Let's assume the beverages you buy are just $2 a day. That's $60 a month, $720 a year, and $36,000 over 50 years. If you invested it at 5%, it would grow to $150,730. Small amounts of money add up to a lot of money.

One potential client came in for a second opinion on his investments. He had $4,000,000 invested in a fee account at a major brokerage firm. The management fees were 1.5% per year; that's $60,000 every year. Maybe 1.5% doesn't seem like a lot, but over 20 years, the total fees are $1,200,000. In 30 years, it's $1,800,000. I knew he could get the same managers and even some better ones for 0.5% per year. That would save him and his wife $40,000 a year, which was a significant amount given that they only wanted $150,000 a year for income. This gave him a new perspective and the power to renegotiate a lower fee.

* * *

LESSONS FROM THE ORCHARD

🍎 Knowing your expenses is a basic step to saving money.

🍎 Concentrating on saving money that is being wasted is almost enough to create your retirement income.

🍎 You can make more money managing your taxes and expenses than you can chasing risky investments.

* * *

What is the most important idea from this chapter you want to apply to your investments?

_____

_____

_____

_____

_____

_____

_____

_____

_____

_____

_____

_____

_____

_____

_____

_____

_____

_____

_____

_____

_____

_____

_____

_____

_____

CHAPTER 6

THE POWER OF
COMPOUNDING INTEREST

We often overlook compounding interest as an investment tool. It's like the law of gravity; it's there but we don't think about it. Compounding interest is called the eighth wonder of the world. It is a mathematical formula that shows how money grows and describes money making money over and over for years.

The Rule of 72

Dividing an interest rate into 72 gives you the number of years it will take to double your money. Six divided into 72 equals 12, so:

> 6% doubles your money in 12 years
> 8% doubles your money in 9 years
> 10% doubles your money in 7.2 years

The real growth of money happens through the reinvestment of the interest or dividends. From this perspective, investment success is easier than people think. It requires patience and discipline, but you will get there. I sometimes needed to remind my brother about investing patience by telling him you don't go into the garden and dig up your seeds to see how they are doing. You just let them grow. It's the same with money. Let the math work for you.

Yields of 8%

When I use 8% as an example of an investment return and someone says, "I'm not getting 8% on my money," I ask them what rate they are paying on their credit card debt. If the credit card companies get a 19% rate from you, your money should be able to earn at least 8% somewhere. Just because you are not getting a good return on your money doesn't mean other people are not. The biggest mistake most investors make is accepting the low rates of return given to the mass market saver.

I know you are skeptical about getting a return of 6%, 8%, or 10%. But if Mastercard and Visa can get 19%, you should be able to get 8%. An average of 8% is a reasonable goal. Some years you will do more, some will do less. You can own stock in companies that are financially strong businesses that pay a dividend of 4–10%. You can loan money to businesses and get 6–8% investing in their bonds. Annuities pay 3–5% tax deferred. There are companies that want to grow at a 20% return on investment. You can look for some of these companies.

Several events led to this different investment strategy and made me realize I was just accepting conventional "wisdom," which wasn't good advice. When I worked for a bank, I learned that banks loan out the same dollar deposited at least 10 times. That means they don't just make 7% on one car loan; they make 70% on 10 car loans.

Then, I worked with a client who managed a corporate division, and he explained his job description as getting a 20% return on investment or selling that business and buying one that will. There are many businesses that want and get a high rate of return on their investment capital. Investors should expect the same.

The final clue was when I saw that one of my client's insurance policies was making five times the amount my money market fund was making. Stockbrokers like me were trained to hate insurance, so this was a complete surprise. These events were the catalyst that inspired me to look for better ways to invest.

Yields on the Whole Portfolio (Not Each Piece)

A realistic goal for a balanced portfolio is an average of 8%. The average annual return of the S&P 500 index since 1957 is roughly 8%. This means that if you get 8% and reinvest it, your money doubles every nine years. This is the growth of a onetime investment of $6,000 invested at 8% without ever investing another dollar at age 25.

This is within the probability of your life expectancy.

Year	
1	$6,000
9	$12,000
18	$24,000
27	$48,000
36	$96,000
45	$192,000
54	$384,000

Besides dividend stocks, you want to find a few companies growing at 10% or even 20% a year. There are few, but they do exist. Most people do not have the time or the experience to search for and find these companies. The best way is to look for an investment manager or mutual fund that manages money this way. Since this has greater risk, you should only invest a portion of your money.

One Crazy Idea Starts with $60,000

What if you aggressively save $60,000 to make a onetime investment and never save another penny? Imagine, at age 30, you and your spouse agree to wait on purchases you want and invest the $60,000 you saved. After saving the $60,000, you'd then be able to buy all the things you want because you planted your orchard and took care of your future. Remember the Rule of 72? The chart below shows $60,000 invested at 8% doubling every nine years. The annual income from $960,000 invested at only 5% would be $48,000 a year.

Year	
1	$ 60,000
9	$120,000
18	$240,000
27	$480,000
36	$960,000

Make a Real Commitment

Think about it. You finance a car and a house you want or even a business. Why not finance the money orchard that will someday pay you an income for life? A serious commitment would be to borrow $60,000 and invest it into your orchard. Then make payments to pay off your investment portfolio loan just like you do with your car or college loan. The best way to do this is with nontaxable accounts. Investing risk free and tax deferred gives the best result. You need an investment expert and a good banker to help design this strategy. You don't want to risk losing money and still have the loan. You should be able to pay it back any time if something unexpected happens, like losing your job or getting sick.

This is a serious commitment and requires extreme discipline and riskless investing. Most people cannot do it.

— • • 🍎 • • —

LESSONS FROM THE ORCHARD

🍎 Earning yields of 8% is a realistic goal.

🍎 Compounding is power that grows your money, which means you don't have to take a lot of risk.

🍎 Investing does not require a lot of time and activity, but it demands patience.

🍎 Time reduces risk. Giving an investment time to grow increases the yield and decreases the effects of market volatility.

🍎 You can own part of a good business. You can own a part of the best businesses in the world.

🍎 You can get income and growth from the same investment.

🍎 Dividend-paying stocks are less volatile. It is easier to ride out the storms when you are getting a check.

— • • 🍎 • • —

What is the most important idea from this chapter you want to apply to your investments?

_____
_____
_____
_____
_____
_____
_____
_____
_____
_____
_____
_____
_____
_____
_____
_____
_____
_____
_____
_____
_____
_____
_____
_____
_____
_____
_____
_____
_____

CHAPTER 7

IDEAS FOR MAKING 8%

These are ideas to explore and consider. It is crucial we know you before we recommend anything.

If you went to a doctor that immediately handed you some pills, you might think, "This is not a good doctor." He never asked about your medical history and didn't do any testing, so how can he prescribe anything with no information about you and your life? He can't. The same is true of any financial advisor. These suggestions are ideas for research to find some interesting possibilities.

Important Framework for These Ideas

Staying with our goal of making an average of 8%, there are several ways to invest. I want to offer you solid evidence it is possible to average 6% to 10% yields on your investment portfolio. Consider these as ideas to expand your investment horizon rather than recommendations. Because of regulatory restrictions, I cannot name specific companies or mutual funds without knowing the specifics of your situation. It is possible to discuss categories that have hundreds of individual companies to choose from. Not naming companies also makes sense because between the time this book was written and when you are reading it, everything could have changed and there might be better ideas available.

Dividend-Paying Stocks

Good dividend stocks are companies that pay dividends between 4 and 10%. Even better if you buy them in a down market when prices are depressed. You can invest in a mutual fund that specializes in these kinds of dividend-paying companies. Fund managers do extensive research to invest in these kinds of companies and then monitor their performance. Currently, there are 281 stocks that pay over 8% dividends and 312 stocks paying over 10%. These stocks can be risky. It really is an area best left to professionals who research and manage this kind of portfolio. It takes a lot of knowledge and experience to choose the best companies.

If you can reach your goal by getting 8%, it is not worth the risk to invest in very high-risk area. It is just like driving down the freeway. Your car can go 100 miles an hour, but eventually you will have an accident. The goal is not to see how fast you can drive; your goal is to get to your destination. The same is true about investing.

Business Development Companies (BDC)

A business development company (BDC) is an organization that loans money to small- and medium-sized companies. Many BDCs trade on the stock exchanges. Usually, the assets of the company borrowing the money back up the loan. Some BDC funds yield between 6 and 14%. The higher yields have more risk. There are significant differences in the companies, so comprehensive research is important before investing.

Open-end Mutual Funds

These are investment companies that anyone can buy with large or small amounts of money. The advantage is that a $25-a-month investment experiences the same growth as a million-dollar investor. There are many investment strategies to choose. In fact, almost every investment strategy already exists in a mutual fund.

Closed-end Funds and Exchange Traded Funds (ETF)

Closed-end funds are mutual funds traded on the stock exchanges. Some very good ones yield 6–8%. They are unlike open-ended funds that are bought or sold at the end of the trading day. Closed-end funds issue a certain number of shares and do not issue more. They can sell at a discount or a premium to the net asset value. This is one of my favorite strategies because of deep discounts in a down market. You can make money in two ways: when the market rises and when the fund price closes the deep discount gap. If the discount is 10%, you are buying a $1,000 portfolio for $900. This type of investing is for experienced investors because the price is volatile.

Annuities

Annuity means annual payment. They have been around since the Roman Empire. The emperor would give an annuity to someone as a reward. Some modern annuities are specifically designed to provide income and growth at the same time. Instead of being linked to a fixed yield like a bond or CD, indexed annuities are linked to different stock indexes. It's like insuring your income stream and keeping the principal safe. It puts a floor under the principal investment so you cannot lose money, and it locks in any growth that you receive during good years. You can choose an annuity that provides safe, predictable income or choose one that maximizes growth depending on your stage of life. I recommend you get annuities from someone licensed in both insurance and securities.

This is one of the most misunderstood investments because the word annuity brings up a lot of negative thoughts. But if you like what it does, do you care what it is called? The main purpose of annuity is to give a safe, predictable income, to keep money safe, and to grow tax deferred. Here are some examples of annuities you might like: a pension, Social Security, and lottery winnings.

You buy an annuity from an insurance company. Some index annuities are a blend of all three trees: protection, income, and growth. There is a safety net that ensures you can't lose your investment and it can grow. Some annuities give you a choice of a guaranteed income for life. You can choose an option for the income to grow for a guaranteed income in the future, even if the investment dollars don't grow as much as you hope. Some indexes are managed portfolios instead of passive indexes, like the S&P 500.

A fixed annuity is another kind of annuity that pays a fixed interest rate. The term can be for one year or many years. This is like a deposit at a bank for a CD that pays more for longer-term commitments.

The advantage of all annuities is the insurance company assumes the risk on the bonds and mortgages it invests in.

Master Limited Partnerships (MLP)

These are usually oil, gas, and pipeline companies that pass the earnings through to investors. Some yields are between 8% and 14%. It is one way to invest in the energy sector of the US economy.

Real Estate Investment Trust (REIT)

A real estate investment trust (REIT) is a company that owns, and in most cases operates, income-producing real estate. REITs own many types of commercial real estate, office and apartment buildings to warehouses, hospitals, shopping centers, hotels, and timberlands. You own a package of buildings that are paying rent; the operating company passes to you after taking a management fee.

Corporate Bonds, Municipal Bonds, and Government Bonds

All bonds are loans to companies or governments for short or long periods of time. The yields are based on the amount of risk and how long the money is invested.

Lessons from the Orchard

🍎 These are ideas. They are like clues where to go looking for better investments.

🍎 Please don't buy any of the investments without further research and preferably advice from a knowledgeable investment professional.

🍎 This is a complex strategy and requires planning, patience, and tremendous discipline.

🍎 While I believe these ideas are good investments, I also know they are not good for everyone. That is why an investment policy is so crucial.

🍎 Your investment policy is a tool to sort through the thousands of options that are in these eight kinds of investments.

What is the most important idea from this chapter you want to apply to your investments?

_____

_____

_____

_____

_____

_____

_____

_____

_____

_____

_____

_____

_____

_____

_____

_____

_____

_____

_____

_____

PART THREE

DANGERS IN THE ORCHARD

CHAPTER 8

INTERNAL OBSTACLES
(OR HOW OUR BRAIN FOOLS US)

The greatest danger we face as investors is our own brain. Sometimes we do not see everything. Sometimes we misinterpret what we think we see. When we understand how our brain works, we can use this knowledge to avoid losing money.

Magic is a perfect way to understand how our brain works and the ways it can fool us. Magicians get us to think we saw something that isn't real and didn't happen. They also fool us into not being able to see what really happened. Think about this for a moment. They trick our brains, even though we go to a magic show expecting to get fooled. If we can be fooled when we know it is happening, it might be a good idea to admit we can also fool ourselves about investment ideas. Wall Street may be the greatest magician of all, with its ability to make money disappear. The greatest trick of all is getting investors to forget it happened.

There are lots of techniques in magic. One of them is misdirection, which means getting you to look somewhere else. Magicians misdirect by telling a story while they do the trick. While your brain is listening to them chat, it can't pay attention to other things that are happening at the same time. They overwhelm your brain verbally so that it can't pay attention to what they are doing. The result is the audience doesn't see everything that is really happening.

Did you ever miss a turn on the freeway because you were talking to someone? Your brain was busy. Have you ever bought a car and start seeing more of them than you ever did before? They were always there, but your brain didn't process the information. The same thing happens when we invest. We see things that aren't there and go down the wrong road loaded with risk. We also miss opportunities that are right in front of us. Our perception of reality causes our actions. If our perception is wrong, reality will teach us a harsh lesson.

Our interpretation of events causes our actions. A different perspective leads to a different interpretation, therefore a different action. Each interpretation seems logical to the person making it. Logical means it is consistent with their perception, not necessarily that it is true. It is important to understand we can and do fool ourselves.

In 2002, my daughter wanted an iPod for graduation. I remember thinking it was going to be a huge moneymaker for Apple, not because of the iPod, but because of all the music they were going to sell. The stock was selling at $10. Since then, there have been several stock splits. Adjusted for the splits, Apple stock grew from $0.45 to $140 in about 20 years. Every day during those two decades, someone sold their Apple stock to someone who bought it. Two different perceptions led to two different courses of action: one person sold, and the other person bought.

Perception Is Not Reality

I remember the first time I heard someone say, "perception is reality" and thinking that it was a ridiculous statement. It was my boss who said it, so I wisely kept my thoughts to myself. Since then, I have heard "perception is reality" many times. I am not sure why people say it, because perception is not reality. Perception can be wrong. People used to perceive Earth as flat and the center of the universe. Common knowledge can be mistaken. Sometimes what everyone knows is true, isn't true.

The process of education is discovering reality and correcting faulty perceptions. If I have the perception that I can jump out the window and fly, reality has a big surprise waiting for me when I reach the ground. Sanity is knowing what is real and requires checking if our perceptions are right. A financial advisor should be able to warn you when you have a wrong idea. The problem is that none of us like to be told we are wrong, but we all need this kind of advice occasionally.

What else can we do to address these gaps in knowledge? We need humility, which means understanding that we might be wrong. Once we adopt an attitude of humility, we will be more likely to look at our decisions from many perspectives. Actions based on reality create better successful outcomes. The more we clarify our perceptions and refine our thoughts, the better our odds of success will be. Therefore, we need a guide or an advisor to help us understand our blind spots. A guide can help us see opportunities we can't see and help us see when we are acting on a mistaken view of reality, which could lead to a costly mistake.

The orchard story introduces a different perspective on financial realities. It gives us a way of thinking outside the box and changes our perception. This is powerful because our perceptions cause our actions. Successful investing requires seeing something before everyone else sees it.

Madness of Crowds

Throughout history, there have been investment bubbles. Robert Shiller of Yale has described bubbles as "a mental illness" with the following characteristics:

- Rapidly increasing prices
- People telling each other stories to justify the reasons for the bubble
- People telling each other how much money they're making
- People feeling envy and regret that they didn't participate
- The news media propagating the bubble

In 1637, during the Dutch "tulip mania," the price of a single tulip skyrocketed to the value of a house. The dot-com bubble burst in March 2000. Before it was over, tech stocks lost $5 trillion of their value. That was the equivalent of half of US GDP that year.

In the 1700s, investors from all walks of life bought and sold shares in the South Sea Company. Among them was a scientist named Sir Isaac Newton. Newton's experience of investing in a bubble is a warning. He lost $4,000,000 adjusted for inflation. If one of the smartest men in history went broke in a financial bubble, will you do better in the latest investment bubble? As a frustrated Newton put it, "I can calculate the movement of the stars, but not the madness of crowds."

Language and Fuzzy Words

Another internal problem is language. Many investment problems are a problem with language. This problem can take the form of fuzzy language or a deliberate misuse of language to manipulate us. The words can sound scientific and intelligent but can be meaningless. We think with words. The more precise the words, the clearer we can see what is real. We see and explain the world using these little pictures called words. Our brains think in these pictures, and if they are out of focus, it is harder to understand what we are seeing and what we should do. Sharpening the definition of the words is like taking a photograph in better focus or from a different angle; it gives us a different perspective.

The financial service industry's language sounds impressive but is not always clear. For example, a current buzzword is fiduciary. Fiduciary applies to any situation where one person places confidence and trust in someone else and seeks that person's help or advice in some matter. Of course, being a fiduciary is important, but just saying the word proves nothing. Bernie Madoff was a fiduciary. This shows words we use to explain investing can inform us or mislead us.

We need words to be as precise as possible. Describing investing as "buying a good business" instead of "investing in the stock market" will significantly improve your results because it improves your understanding of what investment means. During the dotcom bubble, if people asked, is this a good business, they would not have bought most of the stocks they did. Most of them were just ideas, not even close to being a good business.

Diversification

Financial language includes words that are commonly used, like diversification. One client said he was diversified because he owned 50 mutual funds. Someone else said they were diversified because they had money in CDs at 20 different banks. This is not the meaning of diversification, but it is what diversification meant to them. True diversification is investing in different asset classes, like stocks, bonds, real estate, and styles of investment strategies. Another way to diversify is to have your money invested with two or three different investment organizations with different investment philosophies.

Correction

Let's take the word "correction," which is supposed to explain why your stock went down. Correction means the market went down. In everyday English, a correction is when we fix something that went wrong. Using correction in investment contexts is avoiding facing reality. It may sound good, but the word is used to hide the fact that you are losing money. When we invest, we must have a clear grasp of reality. Correction sounds better than crashing.

Shifting definitions make it hard to understand our choices. The industry keeps changing the language. The words change, but there isn't a change to the activity they name: junk bonds became high yield, wrap accounts became fee accounts, stockbrokers became financial consultants and are now wealth managers. People use risk and volatility interchangeably.

Volatility and Risk

We can use the last example of volatility and risk to dive deeper into seeing how language can bring confusion instead of clarity. Investing is risky and dangerous, but risk can be diversified out of your investments, which leaves volatility.

Markets go up and down, and prices constantly change. If you see volatility as a normal ebb and flow of the markets, you are more likely to take advantage of a price drop in a good company. You understand that volatility is the normal movement of the price of a good business. If you think volatility is risk, you are more likely to panic and bail out of a good investment. In orchard language, the ups and downs of the market are like seasons. There is winter and there is summer. Spring and fall are transitions between the two seasons of growth and resting.

---•●🍎●•---

LESSONS FROM THE ORCHARD

🍎 The money orchard helps us understand how our financial landscape works by connecting it to something we already understand. By changing abstract words into images, it paints a concrete picture of investing. It is simple but not simplistic.

🍎 The money orchard is a complete picture of a lifetime investment policy that shows how all the pieces work together.

🍎 The orchard story is not different from traditional financial services concepts. It is describing them through pictures, showing a functional way you loan, own, and protect.

🍎 Money orchard language looks at investing from another angle. It's like a second opinion that changes your understanding about why you save and invest.

🍎 Instead of using traditional words like wealth management, the orchard story helps you understand the financial planning process by changing the language used to explain investments.

---•●🍎●•---

What is the most important idea from this chapter you want to apply to your investments?

_____

_____

_____

_____

_____

_____

_____

_____

_____

_____

_____

_____

_____

_____

_____

_____

_____

_____

_____

_____

_____

_____

_____

_____

CHAPTER 9

EXTERNAL DANGERS

Investing is like a trip into the unknown. The road is not straight or smooth. The money orchard is like a roadmap that you can follow with confidence because you can see the big picture. You may hit some detours, but you can adjust because you have a plan.

The coronavirus pandemic made us all aware of how fragile and unpredictable life can be. Many of the basic things we needed for our lives were unavailable. Stores had shortages of supplies. The flow of our ordinary lives stopped. Most people are not prepared for life to be less than perfect. When the economy shut down, many businesses also shut down. Even a small orchard would have helped many people who lost their income.

These disruptions have given us an opportunity to reevaluate everything and choose different approaches. We need to be prepared for whatever crisis we may have to face. It will be unpredictable. When bad things happen again, we are ready, so the shock is not too disruptive to our lives. Now is the time to prepare.

Inflation

THIS IS EXTREMELY IMPORTANT: The US has a current national debt near $30 trillion and growing. It is essential to understand the impact of inflation on your investments and how it reduces your purchasing power in the future. Since it happens gradually, it seems relatively harmless, but your investment policy must take inflation seriously.

The cost of stamps illustrates the impact of inflation. In 1990, it cost 25 cents to mail a letter compared to 55 cents in 2020. Did the price of stamps go up or did the dollar lose value? Both say the same thing, but the price of stamps going up doesn't sound as bad as the value of the dollar going down. The difference in cost shows the dollar is worth 45% of the 1990 dollar. This happened in your lifetime. It will repeat itself in the next 30 years.

You have experienced 40 years of inflation.

Stamps in 1980 = 15¢

Stamps in 2020 = 55¢

Stamps in 2021 = 58¢

Let's look at the value of $100,000 declining after applying an inflation rate of 3%, which is the historical average. This is the same result the stamps show. This example alone shows the reason a mortgage is a good financial hedge against inflation. You are paying the loan back with cheaper dollars.

3% Inflation Erosion of $100,000 over 30 years

Year End	Inflation Erosion of $100,000
1	$97,000
2	$94,000
3	$91,000
4	$88,000
5	$85,000
6	$83,000
7	$80,000
8	$78,000
9	$76,000
10	$73,000
11	$71,000
12	$69,000
13	$67,000
14	$65,000
15	$63,000
16	$61,000
17	$59,000
18	$57,000
19	$56,000
20	$54,000
21	$52,000
22	$50,000

23	$49,000
24	$48,000
25	$46,000
26	$45,000
27	$43,000
28	$42,000
29	$41,000
30	$40,000

Twenty years later, your money will buy **46% less** than in 2021. After 30 years, it **lost 60%** of its original value. In Chapter 11, I'm going to show you how to use this to your advantage with another financial judo move. You can use inflation to grow your wealth.

The Sinkhole

Debt is one money drains we do to ourselves. It is optional: student loans, credit card debt, car loans, home mortgages. They seem harmless at first but can quickly become slavery to the financial industry. With that said, there are wise uses of debt. Interest paid on home mortgages, investments, even education, or buying and growing a business all make intelligent uses of debt. Housing mortgage is a different type of debt because the interest is deductible, and you have an appreciating asset. It costs more to rent than to own. One very important thing to remember: your sinkhole is someone else's income tree. The interest on your debt is contributing to someone's retirement income. Now you know why you get those credit card applications every week.

When you check out at almost any retail store, the cashier inevitably asks you if you want to open a credit card with them. Amazon will give you $50 to get a card. Airlines will give you $200. Most stores offer a 10% discount on everything you buy today. They know you will buy 30% more with a credit card than you will with cash. In fact, car companies make more money on the credit interest than they do on the car.

The compounding interest in the sinkhole is working against you. Managing taxes and reducing interest payments will make you more money than a brilliant investment. If you stop paying unnecessary interest to banks and credit card companies, it could give you thousands of dollars for your orchard. The average amount of credit card debt in the US is $5,000 with an average rate of 16%. If you were to carry this balance, pay the minimum, and never use the card again, it would take you 166 months to repay it. The total interest paid would be $7,441.

Insurance Deductibles

The storm cloud in the orchard reminds us that life has risks. Some are small, and we can handle them. Others are catastrophic, and the loss would wreck our lives beyond recovery. We need a margin of safety. This is the purpose of insurance.

Medical insurance is one example where you can choose the self-insured part called the deductible. You can choose between a $500, $1,000, or $5,000 deductible. You must pay more each month to get the $500 deductible compared to the $5,000. It's like giving the insurance company extra money, hoping you have enough medical expenses to get your money back.

Instead, if you take the $5,000 deductible and save $2,000 a year, your risk is $3,000 more because you still have the extra $2,000 that you saved. If you have no big medical expenses for three years, you will be financially ahead by $6,000. At this stage, you have money for your orchard that can grow and produce income for the rest of your life. If you are young, the odds of needing a low deductible are low. If you have poor health or are older, you should probably take the lower deductible.

The same idea applies to car insurance, homeowner's insurance, and disability insurance. People save money for their orchard by analyzing the deductibles on different kinds of insurance. Ask your car and home insurance agent to look at your deductibles. It could save you enough money to fund your Roth IRA.

Excessive Fees

Investment fees are one area people struggle to navigate with clarity. Of course, banks, mutual funds, insurance companies, and investment firms need to get paid for their work just like everyone else. Still, what is fair and how do we know? There are thousands of mutual funds and ETFs where you can invest your money. There are investment managers and funds that charge fees ranging from 0.5% to 1.5% per year. Some of the best charge 0.5% to 0.75%.

We learned about compounding interest earlier and saw that fighting for the extra 1% makes your orchard grow faster and will give you a lot more apples in the future. Since we can't predict the future, we don't know what the investment return will be. Lowering the fees is certain to add up to better growth.

Commissions and Fees

When I worked at a trust company, the selling proposition was that we didn't get commissions. Instead, we charged a fee. The idea of a fee/wrap account was paying a flat fee for management. They sold with the logic that "we do better when you do better." However, when the market drops, the investment manager still gets to charge you the fee. For investors with a buy and hold long-term view (which I believe is how people should invest), it would be better to pay a onetime commission and hang on to the investment for years instead of paying a fee year after year. Both fee-based and commission-based approaches are good under the right circumstances.

Investment Losses

Avoiding investment losses is a hidden way to increase the size of a money orchard. One of the cardinal rules for investing is "don't lose money." If you avoid loss in a down market while other people are trying to get back to even, you are stacking positive returns on top of minimal losses. Using the Rule of 72, a $1,000 loss is not just losing $1,000 because you lose the compounding factor as well. The loss is infinite because the money could grow for your children, grandchildren, and great-grandchildren. As we learned earlier, $1,000 invested at 8% would double every nine years. That could create multigenerational wealth. If you are 60 years old, statistically you or your spouse will most likely live to over 90 years old. You might need this money then.

The Financial Industry

Traditional financial services differ in their approach. There are many investment theories about how to invest: day trading, ETF portfolios, fee-based accounts, active and passive investing, indexing, and modern portfolio theory, which is also called asset allocation. Most investment strategies in the financial marketplace will fail you. They are packaged products for the mass market. You are not a mass market investor. You can do something different from what everyone else is doing.

Modern portfolio theory (MPT) states that around 90% of a portfolio's return is from asset allocation, not stock selection. The present trend in financial services is passive investing and indexed funds (a type of mutual fund). It is not necessarily the best way. It is just the one everyone seems to agree upon. Investment fads almost never work out. When everyone is doing the same thing, it usually ends in disaster. In the 1960s, it was the Nifty Fifty. In 1987, it was option trading. In the late 1990s, it was the dot-coms. In 2008, it was real estate and credit default swaps.

All these current investment philosophies ignore the results of investors like Benjamin Graham, John Templeton, and Warren Buffett. In fact, one mutual fund family performance from each of five funds was better than the Vanguard S&P index performance over the same 40 years. What is common to them all was the investment philosophy found in Ben Graham's book, The Intelligent Investor, which we explored in an earlier chapter.

Commoditization

In one of my investment classes, a student shared he was looking for an advisor to help him. He had interviewed five different financial advisors or wealth managers. They all recommended the same strategy and had him fill out a risk profile. Based on the risk profile, they suggested his model portfolio. And for the service, they charged 1% or 1.5% on the assets each year. He asked me, "Couldn't I just do that myself and save the fee?" My answer was "yes you can. And if that is what you want to do, I can show you how to for no charge. We call what they are selling a fee account."

Based on the content and tone of the question, I realized he did not trust financial people, which included me. And that is understandable. So, I asked, "Do you trust Wall Street?" That question was like throwing a match into a room of gasoline. The class all started talking at once. The emotion was intense. Everyone had an opinion on why they did not trust Wall Street. So, I asked why. The next 20 minute discussion was the most interesting class I have ever taught.

The wrap account or fee investment account models are a cookie cutter process. The risk profile questionnaire doesn't work. It looks scientific, but it is not. A few questions cannot measure your risk tolerance and determine how you should invest. The purpose of the money you're investing should determine the investment strategy, not your risk profile or your age. You have different goals, each of which has a different time frame. So, each goal needs a different strategy and probably a different manager.

Each manager has a specific skill set (i.e., bond managers and stock managers). You wouldn't expect them to be experts at both.

One big name money management organization claimed to bring institutional investing to the average person. Part of their presentation on why we should recommend them to clients was that they managed money for foundations and half the billionaires in the world. The error in this logic is this doesn't apply to the average person. The billionaires could lose half of their money and it wouldn't change their lives. Losing just a small amount of money could change the average investor's life forever. When you think about any investment firm's investment strategies compared to your personal situation, it might not fit your life.

Financial Planning

I believe in the financial planning process. I earned the Certified Financial Planner designation in 1987 and did continuing legal education for basic and advanced estate planning. The financial planning process brings all personal finance into a unified and efficient picture. It covers six basic areas: investing, insurance, cash management, employee benefits, estate planning, tax planning, and risk management.

A balance sheet and your income in and income out are the basis of all financial planning. When you go to the bank, you fill out a form that asks for your balance sheet and a profit and loss (P&L) statement. It is an accounting process used to keep track of a business: assets minus liabilities equals net worth. When the financial planner asks for the confidential questionnaire of income expenses and your assets, it's not wrong, but I believe there is more to planning than spreadsheet projections.

Financial planning takes your information and projects it into the future. Unfortunately, it assumes an earnings rate, an inflation rate, your income, the economy's performance, and that nothing bad will happen. It shows a possible future result, but it is predicting a future no one can predict.

Life Expectancy

It is important to plan for at least a 30-year retirement. Life expectancy for a male is about 83 years (I used to think that was my expiration date). But what it means is that, out of 100 men aged 62, half will still be alive at age 83. Once you reach age 83, half will be still alive at age 92. In a family where the husband and wife are both 62 and nonsmokers, statistics show one will be alive at age 92. So, it is necessary to plan for a long life.

———————•●🍎●•———————

Lessons from the Orchard

🍎 Very few people think in terms of balance sheets and income statements.

🍎 Using the money orchard picture helps people understand how different investments work together.

The real purpose of saving and investing is to create income.

🍎 Stories and narratives capture important truths in a simple and powerful way that differs from scientific and mathematical models.

🍎 The story of the tortoise and the hare communicates more than if you were to tell someone that there are no get-rich-quick schemes and success comes from patience and hard work.

🍎 Success comes by plodding along as the tortoise does.

———————•●🍎●•———————

What is the most important idea from this chapter you want to apply to your investments?

_____

_____

_____

_____

_____

_____

_____

_____

_____

_____

_____

_____

_____

_____

_____

_____

_____

_____

_____

_____

_____

_____

_____

_____

_____

_____

_____

_____

_____

PART FOUR

PUTTING IT ALL TOGETHER

CHAPTER 10

SAMPLE PORTFOLIOS

Emergency Fund or Opportunity Fund

It's important to have a cash reserve for emergencies and opportunities. The problem is people are impatient and complain they aren't making any money. When the stock market has a major decline, which it always does about every four or five years, you can buy great companies at bargain prices. For example, let's imagine a $100 stock of a company declines 50% to $50, then it recovers back to $100 for a 100% return. If it took five years to recover, the average return would be 15% per year. That makes holding some cash worthwhile.

Many people do not realize the cash in their life insurance policy can be an emergency fund. They put it in and never touch it. Now that interest rates on money markets and CDs are close to nothing, the cash in my insurance policy earning 5% looks good by comparison. In August 2002, I believed the stock market was close to a bottom. I borrowed the cash from my life insurance policy and invested in a growth fund. Over the next couple of years, my money doubled, and I sold half of the fund and paid the loan back. What most people do not know is the cash in the policy grows the same in the policy even when there is a loan on the policy, which serves as collateral for the loan. When banks wouldn't give Walt Disney a loan, he borrowed the money using his life insurance policy as collateral.

A Portfolio for 2021

The pandemic of 2020 disrupted everyone's life and finances. We learned how fragile the economy and our finances can be. I want to show investment strategies that give people hope they can build a solid financial foundation for their future. There are two enormous obstacles that we face right now: rising inflation and rising taxes.

Roth IRA and 401(k)

A Roth account is the best tax shelter you can find. It grows tax free and comes out tax free. It is a tremendous tool to lower taxes. There is a $6,000 limit per person with an extra allowance of $1,000 for people over 50 years old. You can put in more than the $6,000 limit by converting IRA and 401(k) accounts to a Roth. If you think tax rates are going up, it makes sense to convert now rather than wait to take the money out in a higher tax bracket. One of the best times to convert to a Roth is in a down market. If your investments are down, you convert less money and pay less tax. Then when the market recovers, the gain is tax free.

Remember the tax sinkhole. For most people, they can find the $6,000 they need for the Roth account wasted in interest payments, taxes, and unnecessary expenses. Chapter 5 has ideas to make your money work more efficiently.

Many companies allow for an in-service transfer to an IRA or a Roth IRA. This means you can transfer money out of your retirement plan while still working in your current job.

Most Americans have an adjusted gross income of less than $77,000 adjusted gross income. This means they are in a 12% tax bracket. The tax deduction on IRAs or 401(k)s for them is almost worthless because they are most likely deferring into a high bracket in the future. The tax deduction sounds good today, but in the future, it might be a big mistake. A Roth IRA would be better.

The difference between a pretax deductible retirement account compared to a Roth IRA or Roth 401(k) is the difference between paying tax on the seeds instead of the harvest. You will be ahead in the future paying the low tax and growing the money tax free and taking it out tax free. If you have extra money to save, a Roth or a Roth-type investment is a great tool to save taxes over your lifetime.

One client had a company plan that gave the choice of a traditional deductible 401(k) or a Roth 401(k). The maximum contribution was $17,000. She also had a significant amount of her personal savings in a taxable account. I suggested she put $17,000 of her income into the Roth 401(k), which was almost her whole after-tax check. Her complaint was that she needed to live on that money. I showed her how she could put the money in the Roth and use the $17,000 from other investment accounts

The Money Orchard

for her current lifestyle. This did not affect her day-to-day life, but she was permanently reducing her future taxes. It was just like moving money from one pocket into another. She still had the same amount of money, but with lower taxes.

Financial Roadmap: The Goal

If you want $50,000 coming out tax free, here is what it takes. (For every increment of $50,000 you earn, multiply the calculations; for example, if you make $100,000, multiply everything by 2, $150,000 multiplies by 3, and so on.)

You earn $50,000 per year and want to replace an income of $50,000. You need an orchard of $1,000,000 earning 5% to get $50,000. If your Social Security is $25,000 a year, you only need an orchard of $500,000, earning $25,000 for an income of $50,000 a year.

Saving Plan for $500,000

Use a Roth account to save and grow your money tax free for 30 years. Annually saving $6,000 at 8% for 30 years grows to $679,699. Since you only need $500,000, you have a little cushion for the future.

To create your retirement income, you will invest the $679,699 at a conservative 5% to earn $33,984 a year. If your tax bracket is 25%, this is about the same as making $50,000 taxable income.

With $25,000 from Social Security plus your $33,984, you have a retirement income of $58,984. If you only need to replace your income with $37,675 on a tax-free basis to live, why replace $50,000 in a taxable way so you can continue to pay taxes?

Growth of $65,000 at Different Rates

Below is a sample portfolio in a diversified orchard with the three kinds of trees, investing $65,000 over 30 years and being aggressive with a small portion of your money.

PROTECT	$40,000 at 6%	=	$230,000
LOAN	$20,000 at 8%	=	$201,000
OWN	$5,000 at 12%	=	$150,000
TOTAL GROWTH		=	**$581,000**

This proves you don't need to be aggressive with all your money. (Please understand) I'm using this as a sample pattern, not a specific recommendation for you to follow. Work with a financial professional to design a portfolio using your investment policy.)

If an investment advisor can't grow your money using only 30% of it in the **Growth** tree, why would you think he can do it with all your money? The important point is you should keep some of your money safe in the **Loan** tree and in the **Protect** tree. If you are at a stage in your life when you are living on the income the orchard produces, you need to reduce risk and lock in the income.

Whatever gains you might make through risky investing strategies would not change your life significantly. Losing the money you are living on, however, would change your life forever. A balanced portfolio of stocks and bonds ranges from 70/30 to 30/70. Each individual investor will be comfortable with different allocations based on their knowledge, experience, and skill. This is where you should seek the help of an advisor to tailor a plan for you.

Two Big Mistakes

There are two big investment mistakes: not being diversified enough and being too diversified. Traditional investment design is to blend a portfolio into three basic categories: stocks, bonds, and cash. Using the orchard picture, it becomes easier to see under- or overdiversification and missing trees. Each tree has a specific purpose and works together to create a functioning orchard.

Here is the problem with the traditional way of investing: it makes no sense to have one tree trying to do the work of the other trees. The purpose of the money should determine your investment strategy. Bonds or fixed income have the main purpose of safety and income. The purpose of stocks is growth. Cash is for opportunities that arise. A good stock manager is not an expert in bond investing. A good bond manager is not an expert at equity investing. And I see no reason to pay the same fee for both. I certainly do not want to pay the same fee for cash in my portfolio as I am paying for stock and bond management. Each category—cash, stock, and bond—should have different fees.

The orchard breaks these into their own tree and manages them separately, where it is easier to see how each is performing. Each type of tree has its own experts. You should let the expert in each area manage his kind of tree.

A Good Investment Process

How can you get into the group of people who succeed? Often people ask for a hot tip. In over 40 years in this industry, no one asked me for a good investment process. I want to give you a few suggestions.

First, use the money orchard to organize your financial decisions. Write your investment policy.

Second, join or start an investment community with people who are serious about creating financial self-reliance. Sometimes what seems like a fantastic idea in your head sounds dumb when you write it down or say it to someone else. You will also get investment ideas from other people.

In the investment world, there are investors who try to do it themselves. This amazes me. Investment managers have staff and researchers to help them find good companies to invest in. Most people do not have the money or access to get the same quality of investment research.

Every company in America has a board of directors made up of people with different perspectives to help guide the CEO and management team. Investors need a way to get new insights. We all have blind spots. We need someone who can function just like a board of directors for our financial lives.

Third, find a financial professional who is a holistic advisor. They will help you see a different perspective. One prospective investor interviewed me and several other managers. During our conversation, I asked him the question, "If I give you advice, will you listen to me?" He paused and thought about it for quite a while. Then he said, "That is a good question." I wasn't sure he would. You need to find someone who knows you and you trust to give ideas that apply to your life. You need to know and trust the advisor as well, not with blind trust, but earned trust.

Lessons from the Orchard

Basic Rules for Investing:

🍎 Protect a significant portion of your wealth from loss.

🍎 If you can't grow your money with 30% of your assets, why do you think you can do it with all of it?

🍎 Diversify by using all three kinds of trees. The orchard is an organic unit working together.

🍎 Avoid taxes.

🍎 Use Roth accounts and other tax-deferred strategies.

🍎 Hire a guide to help you navigate the investment seas.

What is the most important idea from this chapter you want to apply to your investments?

_____

_____

_____

_____

_____

_____

_____

_____

_____

_____

_____

_____

_____

_____

_____

_____

_____

_____

_____

_____

_____

_____

_____

_____

CHAPTER 11

A UNIQUE STRATEGY

Use a Mortgage as a Triple Hedge Against Inflation

The hedge against inflation happens in three ways.

1. The loan is being paid back with cheaper deflated dollars.
2. **The house is appreciating because of inflation.**
3. The loan interest is locked in at a low rate and the investment account's yield is higher.

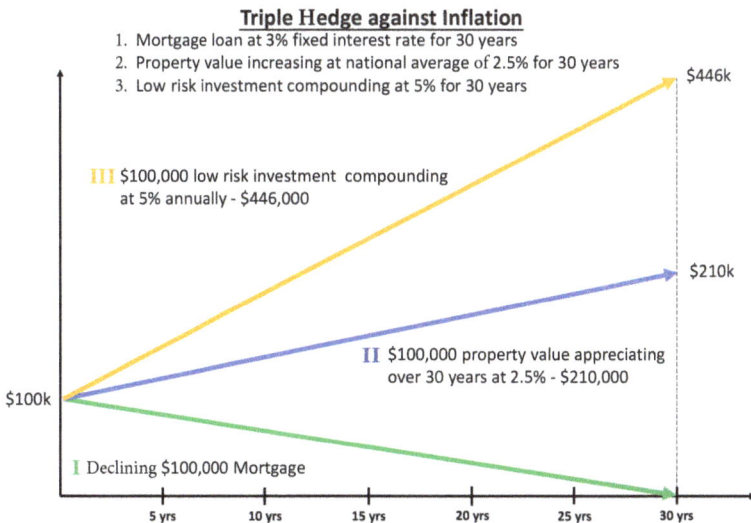

Triple Hedge against Inflation
1. Mortgage loan at 3% fixed interest rate for 30 years
2. Property value increasing at national average of 2.5% for 30 years
3. Low risk investment compounding at 5% for 30 years

$446k

III $100,000 low risk investment compounding at 5% annually - $446,000

$210k

II $100,000 property value appreciating over 30 years at 2.5% - $210,000

$100k

I Declining $100,000 Mortgage

5 yrs   10 yrs   15 yrs   20 yrs   25 yrs   30 yrs

You know about reverse mortgages from the ads on TV. This hedging idea is a similar strategy, but instead of spending the equity, you use the money to create an income without spending the principle. You create another money orchard tree to produce income.

This is an Important Strategy

I believe $30 trillion US debt will cause inflation to increase. History proves this. So, if you use this hedging strategy, you have more money and a paid-up house. The money grows by compounding while the mortgage continues to get smaller and smaller.

People debate whether it is preferable to have your house paid for or to have a mortgage and invest the money. Owning your house paid up is psychologically comforting. But money in a house is a non-income–producing asset. There is no return on the money. It is virtually dead money. Any growth in house value is appreciation, which is the same for a paid-up house or a house with a mortgage.

People say, "I don't want to be in debt." Behind their words is often a misunderstanding of debt. If you have a house worth $300,000 and a mortgage of $300,000, you are not in debt. Your house is an asset that offsets the mortgage debt. In financial language, this is leverage. It is a wise use of debt to make money.

You should be able to pay off your mortgage but have the money growing in a safe no-risk investment. Instead of cutting down the apple tree to pay for the house, we are using the apples from the tree to make the payment on the house.

The math below shows that if you borrow the money at 3% and invest it for 5%, you are gaining 2% per year. This adds up to a lot of money over several years. And if interest rates rise to 8% (and they will someday), you have locked in paying 3% but earning a much higher rate of return. This strategy involves arbitraging the IRS tax code, leveraging the banking industry, using compounding interest to your advantage, and creating an inflation hedge.

If you borrow $100,000 at 3% and invest at 5%, the monthly payment of principal and interest is $421.60, and the annual payment is $5,059.25. The $2,971.44 interest is deductible from income taxes. You can pay the loan with the interest earned by investment, but the growth will be slower. Charts full of numbers are difficult to read, so I am going to break down each calculation separately. Then at the end we can put them together.

The Inflation Erosion on $100,000

The 100-year historical average of inflation is 3%. In 30 years, $100,000 will buy only $40,000 worth of stuff. The value of your money is cut in half in less than 30 years. The other way to understand this is you are paying your loan with cheaper dollars every year. Your work income should increase because of inflation. This is the effect of 3% inflation on a $100,000 loan. See Chapter 9 for the inflation chart.

Declining Loan and Interest Paid for 30 Years

Here are the declining payments on a $100,000 home loan. Each year, the interest paid is less and the loan balance is continuing to decrease compared to investing the $100,000 at 5% growing it into a significant asset.

Year	Declining Loan	Interest Paid
1	$100,000	$2,971
2	$97,912	$2,907
3	$95,760	$2,842
4	$93,544	$2,775
5	$91,260	$2,705
6	$88,906	$2,634
7	$86,481	$2,5604
8	$83,982	$2,484
9	$81,407	$2,405
10	$78,753	$2,325
11	$76,019	$2,242
12	$73,202	$2,156
13	$70,299	$2,068
14	$67,308	$1,977
15	$64,226	$1,883
16	$61,050	$1,786
17	$57,778	$1,687
18	$54,406	$1,584
19	$50,931	$1,478
20	$47,351	$1,370
21	$43,662	$1,257
22	$39,860	$1,142
23	$35,943	$1,023
24	$31,907	$900
25	$27,748	$773
26	$23,463	$643
27	$19,047	$509
28	$14,497	$370
29	$9,809	$228
30	$4,977	$81

In the first year, you earn enough to pay the mortgage payment. By the 15th year, you are making two times the amount of the interest payments. If interest rates rise in the future—and they will—you will make more money than the chart below is showing. You have locked in the loan cost at 3% with low interest rates and the interest rate will increase.

Year	Grows to	Each Year Earns
1	$105,000	$5,000
5	$128,000	$6,400
10	$163,000	$8,150
15	$208,000	$10,400
20	$265,000	$13,250
25	$339,000	$16,950
30	$432,194	$21,600

Summary

At the end of 30 years, your home is paid off and your investment account is $432,194, giving you an additional income of $21,600 a year for the rest of your life. At 3% inflation, the house appreciated to about $300,000 and you now have no mortgage. In comparison, if you save $5,059 each year at 5% for 30 years, you will earn $374,785 instead of $432,194.

The reason for the difference is you have more money compounding from the very beginning. Between the 10th and 11th years, you could take out cash from the investment, pay off the loan, and let the balance of the investment account continue to grow. Using a no-risk tax-deferred investment over 30 years in a Roth IRA or an annuity is a good example of an investment that works best because of tax deferral.

Year	LOAN	Interest Paid	5% Growth	Each Year Earns
1	$100,000	$2,971.44	$105,000	$5,000
5	$91,260	$2,705.62	$128,000	$6,400
10	$78,753	$2,325.21	$163,000	$8,150
15	$64,226	$1,883.37	$208,000	$10,400
20	$47,351	$1,370.08	$265,000	$13,250
25	$27,748	$773.87	$339,000	$16,950
30	$4,977	$81.26	$432,194	$21,600

Leverage as a Financial Tool

Many stores where you shop do not own the buildings. Think about Walgreens, CVS, Federal Express, Amazon distribution centers, Walmart, hotels, and grocery stores. They have calculated that the business can get a higher return on investments than it would with cash tied up in a building, earning nothing. They rent using a triple net lease. With a triple net lease, the tenant rents the building and agrees to pay the property expenses, such as real estate taxes, building insurance, and maintenance, and utilities. Investor that own the building get income from the property. An advanced investor should be able to use this same strategy with their home.

Many businesses, with staffs of CPAs and financial people, decide that they can use the company's cash to make more money than owning the building. It makes the same sense for individual investors to consider the same strategy for themselves.

Earlier in the book, I made two statements: 1) the purpose of Wall Street is to raise money for businesses and 2) you can invest in real estate investment trusts (REIT) for income. These are alternative investments that Wall Street creates and sells. But if you try to take money out of your house to invest, they will not let you.

If they know you are doing this, they will probably not approve the account. Yet they will let you have a margin account with your stocks and bonds and borrow 50% more money as collateral to invest in more stocks that can go down. This is not logical. You are more likely to get hurt by the margin loan because market volatility will almost always cause you to lose in a down market.

I want to be give a strong warning. Everyone should not use this strategy! It is usually a mistake to borrow money to invest in stocks. This mortgage strategy of a triple hedge against inflation should only be invested in riskless investments.

If this strategy makes sense for you to use, you must use professional advisors to help you. You need a CPA for tax advice and a banker to help you with the right mortgage. Take no investment risk! The rule is you should be able to pay off your house at any time. I believe even in retirement you should have a mortgage because of the tax deduction and the inflation hedge a house gives. But you should have investments equal to the mortgage earning more than the cost of the mortgage payments. A perfect goal is to have a Roth IRA of $300,000 yielding 5% or more and a mortgage of $300,000 with a rate of 3%.

---•●🍎●•---

Lessons from the Orchard

🍎 A mortgage can be a powerful financial tool.

🍎 There is a wise use of debt and a foolish use of debt.

🍎 Businesses use their assets of real estate equity to grow their income.

🍎 Reverse mortgages are one use of debt for retirement income.

Extra Warning

There is a danger with this strategy, which is spending the money instead of investing it. The problem is most people will use the cash from the home to spend on their lifestyle or will invest the money where there is a risk of losing. This strategy must be implemented with a riskless investment. It requires disciplined investing with a fixed interest rate on the loan and the money in a tax-deferred investment with no risk of losing the money.

---•●🍎●•---

What is the most important idea from this chapter you want to apply to your investments?

_____

_____

_____

_____

_____

_____

_____

_____

_____

_____

_____

_____

_____

_____

_____

_____

_____

_____

_____

_____

_____

_____

_____

_____

_____

_____

CHAPTER 12

WHAT IS YOUR INVESTMENT TYPE?

The first step to creating a successful investment strategy is to discover your investment personality. Knowing your investment personality gives you confidence your investment strategy and personality match. Then you'll choose good investments and have the conviction to hang on to them.

Your Investment Type

You have a dominant investment personality that you are most comfortable using. When you are investing, you will use a combination of all three investment types to greater or lesser degrees based on the purpose of the money invested. When there is stress on your financial situation, you will retreat to your dominant type.

Air Traffic Controller: Don't crash.
The financial industry describes this type as investing for safety.

This investment type starts with the belief that preventing crashes is the basis of good investing. Managing risk is important for all investment personalities. The advantage of this type is you are not falling behind and needing to catch up. You are steadily growing your net worth with less market volatility and less stress because of market cycles. The disadvantage is you may be too cautious and be losing purchasing power to inflation. This is the best strategy for money with a short time frame for when you need to use the money.

Commercial Airline Pilot: Get there safely and on time.
The financial industry describes this type as investing for income and growth.

This investment type is focused on arriving at the destination safely and on time with a comfortable journey. The advantage of this type is the predictability of the results. It is a middle-of-the-road approach between the air traffic controller and the test pilot. The disadvantage of this type is you might miss some opportunities. This is the best approach for investing when you have time to let the investments grow.

Test Pilot: Push the boundaries safely.
The financial industry describes this type as investing for growth.

This investment type thrives on the adventure of finding new investment ideas and enjoys the process. The advantage of this type is finding businesses that are growing. The disadvantage is the likelihood of significant losses. This approach requires time and research to increase the chances of success. Most investors would benefit by finding a specialty manager or fund that invests in this way rather than investing on their own.

Why is this important?

As a part of their fiduciary duty, retirement plans, endowment funds, mutual funds, and trust accounts have a written investment policy. The purpose is to guide and restrict the managers to a specific goal to keep the money safe and growing at a realistic rate of return. One of the most important reasons for having a written investment policy is to avoid disastrous losses. Another is to have a tool to choose good investments.

An investment policy is important because it will keep you on the right road and avoid dead ends. Your investment personality is the first step to finding an investment strategy that you can follow with confidence. Your answers to the quiz questions are a beginning to writing your investment policy. It can be as simple as one sheet of paper with a few brief sentences or more detailed, depending on the amount of assets you are investing.

Action Step: Write an investment policy based on your investment personality. You will have at least two policies, one for your safe money and the other for your growth money. Over time and market cycles, you will increase and decrease the percentages of each.

A Fence Around Your Money

An investment policy is like a fence around your money to collect good ideas and keep the bad ideas out. Unfortunately, very few investors have a written investment policy. The basic structure is:

Purpose and Aim
Overview of the plan
Investment guidelines for selecting securities and
managers and types of investments
Description of duties and responsibilities and reporting
requirements
Personal situation Restrictions
Key benchmarks for monitoring investments

There are two basic investment categories: safety and growth. You
are always balancing between two goals of protecting money and
growing money. You can't succeed with a strategy that doesn't fit
you. When the economy is growing and the stock market is going
up, it is easy to get caught up in the excitement and get pulled
beyond your comfort range when investing. Your investment
profile is your core that you will fall back on when under market
stress. If you stick with your basic personality, you will not get
trapped in strategies that don't work.

Your policy needs to adjust based on the purpose of the
investment. You need two policies: one for fixed income and the
other for equity investments.

Your age also determines the percentages of which investment
category you use. If you are retired or about to retire, your goal
will change from growth to protecting your income for the rest
of your life. You will still want growth, but with a smaller portion
of your investment dollars at risk. At this stage of life, you want
to protect your income.

If you are younger, time reduces the risk of your investments. A 10-year time horizon increases the odds of success and almost eliminates the risk in a diversified portfolio. In one year, you can win or lose on any investment, but if the investment strategy is sound, you take advantage of time as an investment tool. You can use a greater percentage of growth and aggressive growth strategies. But you must be able to stick to the strategy for a period of years for this to work.

What I would do differently if I could go back in time!

I have worked in the financial service industry for 42 years. Recently, one of my customers asked, *"What would you do differently if you could go back and change anything?"*

In 1980, my core investment personality was an ITP with no skills or experience. It is why I wrote *The Money Orchard* book about what I wish I had known then. I had $100,00 to invest.

1.0 I would have bought 30-year treasury bonds that in early 1980s had yields of 14%. At the time, I did not know that the historical return of the stock market was only 9.2%.

2.0 I would have invested the income from the treasury bonds in a large cap value mutual fund and a small cap fund using dollar cost averaging. The mutual funds would have grown to be an unbelievable $23 million.

I should have **ignored** short-term trading and buying options. In 1986, I owned 10,000 shares of Intel stock, which I sold for a $4,000 profit. You know the Wall Street piece of wisdom, "you can never go broke taking a profit." That trade could have become $1.3 million. You learned in the book the stock exchanges make money by moving it around. They have no incentive to encourage long term investing.

3.0 My major goal would be to create an income portfolio using income and growth investments in the right combination.

APPENDIX I

My Personal Investment Policy

My work is the way I make money in a predictable way. My financial growth comes from working in my business and serving people with my unique abilities. I want to focus my efforts on my work. My investments are a place to store money and get reasonable growth.

My personal goal is to simplify my life and reduce stress because of money and investments. Another goal of my investment policy is to reduce a few of the layers of fees and taxes. I want my retirement income from investments to be $10,000 a month after taxes and to save whatever is above this amount. At retirement, I want the income to be 100% safe and predictable with no market risk.

Invest in value stock mutual funds for growth. Use index annuities as a bond substitute for safety and income. Use 5% to 10% of my assets in a small cap index for aggressive growth. Use Roth IRAs as much as possible. Rarely invest in individual stocks.

Always have a mortgage on my home but have the same amount of cash in my index life policy that could pay off the house.

I want to hold my assets at three different organizations so that only 1/3 is held at one institution. This diversifies investment styles and investment philosophies. Stock managers should not invest in bonds since that objective is accomplished by a bond manager. They can keep a cash reserve in short-term money markets or CDs. There are two portfolios are separated into equity managed by a stock expert and fixed income managed by a bond expert.

This really is my investment policy. Brief enough to understand and detailed just enough to limit major mistakes. Even though my goal for the total portfolio is 8% over a long period. It's just a goal. I cannot control what the economy will give.

APPENDIX II

The Parable of the Apple Tree: The Original Orchard Story
Ray Lyne of Lifestyle Giving

In the beginning, God created the apple tree. He said to the man and woman: "I give you this tree. I'll teach you how to take care of my tree. I'll show you how to fertilize it and how to prune it. I'll send the sunshine and the rain and together we will grow a beautiful apple tree. The tree will produce blossoms and those blossoms will become food you can eat. Inside you'll find seeds. I will teach you to take those seeds and plant them."

They did as God instructed. They pruned and fertilized, and God sent the sunshine and the rain. And soon they had a beautiful orchard producing red, shiny, delicious apples.

We call that stewardship.

Man and woman had children. They taught their children to grow their own apple trees. They had a country full of apple orchards. But mankind argued with each other about their orchards and who got the apples. They went to God and asked him to explain the rules. God said, "It is not good that people should live this way." So, he sent kings and judges to be in charge.

We call that government Caesar.

The kings did their job, the judges did their job, and peace returned to their country. Then Caesar came to the people and said, "HEY, we need some apples to run the kingdom."

We call that income tax.

People didn't like it...just like we don't like taxes now. But they understood it takes money to run the government. People knew they could live with any income tax system, so long as they had enough apples left over to eat. Every year, they would go into the apple orchard and pick 100 bushels of apples. Caesar would take his 30 bushels of apples, but the family still had enough left over to eat. They could live with that system because next year they would pick another 100 bushels of apples.

Then the woman noticed there was a surplus of apples in their country and there were other countries that didn't have enough apples to eat. She decided to sell the apple orchard and build a packing company and ship the extra apples to countries that didn't have enough apples. But you know what happened? When man and woman sold their apple orchard, Caesar came and cut down one out of every four trees.

We call that a capital gains tax.

Then man and woman realized something different had happened. When Caesar took a third of the apples as an income tax, they went back into the orchard the next year and picked another 100 bushels of apples. But when Caesar cut down the trees, there were 25% fewer apples. One day, their neighbor died. And Caesar came and cut down half his apple trees.

We call that an estate tax.

The man said to Caesar, "Caesar, don't you understand? There are only two things you can do with an apple tree. You can grow apples, or you can cut them down and burn it as firewood."

Sometimes Caesar cuts down trees and burns them as firewood when it isn't even cold outside.

The man said, "Caesar, those are not your trees. Those are God's trees. God has put us here as caretakers of those trees. I'm going to build a fence around my orchard and I'm not going to give you a key. You can stand at the gate and take some of the apples, but you cannot cut down God's trees.

We call the fence a trust.

Conclusion

The orchard is a story about life. The truly valuable things in life are things money can't buy. Family, friends, love for our country, and your values are irreplaceable. Life is about becoming the best human possible, the best father, mother, husband, wife, friend, and citizen. It is about becoming the person God made you to become and to experience and enjoy the world He made.

APPENDIX III

A Summary of The Money Orchard's New Perspective

• The work tree and orchard trees show that money is a byproduct of serving people by giving something they need or want. The perfect job is using your individual talents to make the world a better place by serving with your unique abilities.

• Investing is finding a good business that serves people by giving them something they need or want.

• Capital is a different kind of money. It is money that has been saved and invested in a business, land, or a financial asset that can make an income. If the business does not serve people, it will go out of business. In the orchard language, the tree will die.

• We can make our future starting in the present. It starts with a dream of what we want. Then we need to ignore everything that tells us we can't achieve it. Then we need to learn how to take the right steps to make our vision of the future come true.

• Life is like the weather; the sun doesn't always shine. We need to prepare for unpredictable events. Risk management is as important as investing in good businesses.

• There are obstacles to our financial success. Managing the risks is based on recognizing what the risks and dangers are.

• Our understanding of the world and events is limited. We need the knowledge and insights of other people to make good decisions.

• We need humility. The human brain is designed in a way that has perception limits. We all have blind spots. We need to realize we might not be the geniuses we think we are.

• The purpose of investing is not collecting assets (trees). The reason for saving and investing is to create income. You could own $5,000,000 worth of gold and have no income.

• Financial service professionals are tree salesmen. There is nothing wrong with this. Sometimes the trees are exactly what we need. Investors need a comprehensive process, so everything is coordinated to work efficiently.

• Financial service companies don't exist primarily to help investors. Banks make loans, and Wall Street raises money for businesses.

• History shows us patterns that repeat themselves so we can avoid the same mistakes.

• The Money Orchard adds unique contributions to the conversation about personal finance.

• It helps you find money you don't know you are losing so you can invest.

• It shows some unique ways to reposition assets for safety, growth, and income.

• Creates the concept of the two horizons of personal and corporate finance.

• Explains financial services functionally instead of bank, insurance, and investment.

• The orchard shows people and businesses make money by serving people. Money is a byproduct of service.

• The orchard shows there are two kinds of money: capital & income.

• It shows capitalism is not evil. It is money making money by serving people's needs and wants.

• A way to identify a good business is by asking this question. **Does the business serve people by giving them something they need or want?**

• Identifies perception and language as causes of failure in the investment process.

• Reframes the goal from accumulating assets to the goal of creating income.

• Changes the investment goal from investing in the stock market to buying a good business.

• Connecting your sinkhole (debt) to the loan tree (someone else's loan tree) shows both are compounding interest but in different directions.

• Shows the mistake of cutting down a tree (spending capital) and losing apples (income) forever.

Contact us at: https://zaderaka.com

ABOUT THE AUTHOR

Dennis**Zaderaka**

Deep financial knowledge with decades of experience

Dennis Zaderaka has 42 years of experience as a financial advisor. He has developed a wide range of experience in all areas of the financial industry, banks, trust companies, estate planning, insurance, and investment companies.

Going beyond standard financial industry training, Dennis got specialized knowledge at the College of Financial Planning Denver 1987 CFP and Cannon Financial/Northwestern Law School: 32 hours of Basic and Advanced Estate Planning Continuing Education.

Born in Moline, Illinois, he attended Bethel University, Bethel Seminary, Wheaton Graduate School, and the University of Nottingham.

In addition to advising individuals on investments and estate planning, Dennis teaches financial literacy courses as an employee benefit. Past companies include the US Army Reserve, Medtronic, AT&T Bell Labs, AT&T Hispanic Conference, St. Jude Medical, Dow AgroSciences, Sherman Hospital, Apogee Enterprises, Gary-Wheaton Bank, and others.

He currently lives in Phoenix, Arizona after moving from Wheaton, Illinois.

www.ingramcontent.com/pod-product-compliance
Lightning Source LLC
Chambersburg PA
CBHW040925210326
41597CB00030B/5182